Taking Jesus Seriously

Buddhist Meditation for Christians

John Cowan

LITURGICAL PRESS
Collegeville, Minnesota

www.litpress.org

Cover design by Greg Becker

1	2	3	4	5	6	7	8

Library of Congress Cataloging-in-Publication Data

Cowan, John, 1935–
    Taking Jesus seriously : Buddhist meditation for Christians /
John Cowan.
        p. cm.
    Includes bibliographical references and index.
    ISBN 0-8146-2758-7 (alk. paper)
    1. Christianity and other religions—Buddhism. 2. Buddhism—
Relations—Christianity. 3. Meditation—Buddhism. I. Title.
BR128.B8C69 2004
248.3'4—dc21

                                                    2003047490

Contents

Now with you is wisdom, who knows your works
and was present when you made the world;
who understands what is pleasing in your eyes
and what is conformable with your commands.

Send her forth from your holy heavens
And from your glorious throne dispatch her
That she may be with me and work with me,
That I may know what is your pleasure.

For she knows and understands all things,
And will guide me discreetly in my affairs
And safeguard me by her glory.

(Wis 9:9-11)

Prelude

This morning I woke puzzled about how I was to begin this book. My morning meditation was filled with calculations about the cleverest approach to beginning, the one assuring memorable reviews and multi-sales. Is it not ironic that I burned my meditation period calculating how to design a book on meditation reinforcing my sense of being a person separate and autonomous? After breakfast and during the morning prayer that I must pray in answer to a vow made forty years ago, the church placed on my lips these words, "Lord, today may I be of service to your people."

I pray that that becomes my guiding sentiment.

But my need to be a person separate and distinct being what it is and I being who I am, perhaps the most I can pray for is that as I serve my sense of self by attempting to understand something not very understandable, I may at the same time serve the Lord's people.

All human formation is the result of many interacting forces, flowing through literally hordes of people. Out of the vortex I pluck some names to express my gratitude for this aspect of my unusually happy life. Faye Berton, erstwhile my yoga teacher, later my friend, wiser in the ways of the East than I will ever be. Ellen Hufschmidt who one day said that I should attend a Buddhist retreat, launching the practice that I present here. Khamala Masters and Steve Armstrong, my principal teachers of the way that goes nowhere. The old men of the Roman Catholic Seminary system, some of whom exemplified the Jesus that I still follow.

My mother who sat in meditation every day with a cup of coffee for her focal point and did not know what meditation was.

The writers, principally: Shunryu Suzuki, Thomas Merton, Jean Klein. The Buddhists that I follow are primarily from the *vipassana* tradition. That tradition is the slow and gentle path to gradual awakening. Secondarily, I am deeply influenced by the Zen tradition. And then also by some writers and teachers from the yogic traditions.

I rely greatly on the scripture scholars of the Jesus seminar for the authenticity of the sayings of Jesus. This is a group of at its largest two hundred scholars who specialize in studying the Christian Gospels. They are required to have extensive academic credentials, but other than that there are no qualifications such as denomination or even degree of conservatism or liberalism. They have devoted several years in a couple of meetings a year to defining what in the Gospels it is that Jesus said and what is simply attributed to him by the later Christian community. About seventy-five of these scholars have signed the two major reports.

I note that the field of scripture scholarship is in dispute. My opinion is that on the whole the positions taken by these scholars will be accepted in time. I use them with minimal argument. I am not equipped to join the debate. I accept as a layman one set of opinions over another because they resonate to my understanding of reality. The quotations I will use come from *The Gospel of Jesus,* an assembly of texts created by the Jesus scholars and the translation I use is from the "Scholars version," a translation prepared by this same seminar. When I refer to the sayings of Jesus, I will use a number in parentheses to indicate what chapter of *The Gospel of Jesus* I am citing.

My dependency on these scholars and my gratitude should be evident.

At the same time, I sometimes suspect that a specific set of positions reflect not their scholarship but their emotional bias and their spiritual inadequacies as, of course, will my positions, and the positions of anyone else. The refining fire of mother time will fix this in a decade or two. For now I plow ahead.

As you read you may be reluctant to set aside certain sayings as not having been said by Jesus. Indeed, you may come aware that I believe fewer of the doctrines of Christianity than you do or believe them in a different way. This need not interfere with your study of meditation. As long as you agree that Jesus said what my directions depend on his having said, and as long as you find palatable the Christian teachings that I assert, you need not be bothered by what I might deny if you confronted me with a direct question.

A student wrote: "The trouble with theologies is that they are words strung together and professed as truths. Once one has meditated deep enough and really touched the core of his or her being, the 'Silence' within obviates words, which only veil the truth, i.e., our oneness with God. 'The letter killeth, the Spirit giveth life.' Words are divisive, whereas the Spirit unites. Cut through the beliefs and concepts that we carry around us, and what we will find is the underlying 'nothingness,' the 'vacuum into which God rushes.'"

Since an author frequently has no idea what else his readers might find helpful, I have enlisted the assistance of a group of students who have submitted questions and comments as they worked their way through the chapters in class. The voices come from lawyers, doctors, acupuncturists, executives, housewives, and some others who attend St. Luke's in Hastings, St. Martha and Mary in Eagan, St. Anne's in Sunfish Lake, the Cathedral of St. Mark in Minneapolis, St. Christopher's in Roseville, and the University Episcopal Center. These are all Episcopal Churches in Minnesota. These questions and comments in slightly edited form occur at the end of relevant chapters. This book bears witness to the fact that no man is an island. These people have enriched these pages with their questions and frequently their answers.

Sometimes I will repeat a piece of information because the students raise the question before I intended to answer it. So I answer it when they raise it, and I say it again where it fits into my order. Sometimes they ask again what I thought I had explained adequately previously. In those cases I put the question and answer in the text where it occurred during class, assuming the first time must have not been as definitive as I thought. Most of these topics are subtle enough that it does not hurt to hear them twice. I have heard some of them ten thousand times and am beginning to understand them as I write them.

I remind my readers that God tasks one of you with writing a better book on this subject but not yet, please. The self-confidence required to initiate this manuscript is obvious. Let no one think this violet is blushing. At the same time, before my inadequacies are pointed out by others, allow me to state that I am neither a Scripture scholar nor a true expert in Buddhist meditation. My Buddhist friends correct me often (sometimes when I am quoting one of them to another).

Over the door of my office hangs the sign stolen from Christ Church, Frontenac, after my tenure in that minuscule parish. It says simply: "John Cowan, Parish Priest." That is all I am and all I have been through several careers.

What you are receiving here is the accumulated wisdom of one parish priest who has worked in business for twenty-five years, lived in a monastic environment for twelve years, served a parish for thirteen years. He draws on Christian teaching, Buddhist teaching, volumes of psychology, and years of human relations training, just one highly educated pilgrim dumping his relevant knowledge in the thrift shop of literature for other pilgrims to pick over and make their own what pleases them.

There is of course no such thing as "Buddhist meditation for Christians." Once I begin to adapt what I have learned from the Buddhists to a Christian mind set, it is no longer Buddhist. I infect pure Buddhism with my sense of my deepest self as a condensation of the Divine, with my optimism for human destiny, and with my experience of a Divine Presence. A pure Buddhist would expect to discover no self at all, no destiny other than being and a oneness with all beyond a Divine Presence. Be warned and watchful of these major differences.

At a very subtle level, notice that while I teach methods for finding the space between the Divine Condensation in your soul and all the ordinary push and pull of ordinary life I never deny the reality of ordinary life. As a Christian and as an Anglican I am convinced that the Divine is incarnate and becoming incarnate. I take seriously thoughts and feelings, desires, jet planes, government organization, tall buildings, and waves of grain. That is where God shall work and the Divine Presence shall rest. However, I attack the delusion that they are all that exists and lift up the awareness of God in you as discernable from the racket that the push and pull creates.

If you would like to contact me as of January 2004 my e-mail address is sittingjohn@aol.com.

This amazing simplification comes when we "center down," when life is lived with singleness of eye from a holy Center where the breath and stillness of Eternity are heavy upon us and we are wholly yielded to Him. Some of you know this holy, recreating Center of eternal peace and joy and live in it day and night. Some of you may see it over the margin and wistfully long to slip into that amazing Center where the soul is at home with God. Be very faithful to that wistful longing. It is the Eternal Goodness calling you to return Home, to feed upon green pastures and walk beside still waters and live in the peace of the Shepherd's presence. It is the life beyond fevered strain. We are called beyond strain, to peace and power and joy and love and thorough abandonment of self. We are called to put our hands trustingly in His hand and walk the holy way, in no anxiety assuredly resting in Him.

A Testament of Devotion, Thomas R. Kelly

1

The Reign of God, Escaping Delusion

Take Jesus Seriously

(God's imperial rule) will not come by watching for it. It will not be said, "Look here it is!" or "Look over there!" Rather, the Father's imperial rule is spread out upon the earth, and people don't see it (15).

Explanation

A life of extraordinary joy is available to you. That is what Jesus taught. This may not have been what you were taught in his name, and it is certainly not what I was taught.

From childhood on my church ingrained in me that life would be a miserable experience, "a valley of tears." If I accepted God's rules, a set of laws that blocked me from the most pleasurable experiences of life, and took on the chin bravely the onslaughts of his will, I would, after death, be rewarded. At the same time, those who had lived with hedonistic pleasure would be punished for giving in to their base animal instincts. I would have much preferred a message that presented instant happiness without all this painful waiting. Why did my ancestors cheat me out of it?

After his death the message of Jesus was passed through generations and various cultures by word of mouth. The first written account we have of what purports to be his sayings was written fifty years after his death. That is the Gospel of Mark.

The Gospel of John was written eighty years after he died. The Nicene Creed, the standard proclamation of faith among Christian denominations was written three hundred years after his death. His original companions wrote none of these.

At best our records captured an oral tradition in a community started by an original disciple. More often than not this community was situated in a place far distant from Jesus' homeland. These Christians held a set of philosophical premises about life that Jesus never knew. The great apostle, Paul of Tarsus, never met Jesus and was not trained by someone who had. He spread Christianity without knowing Jesus personally. He spoke with the confidence of his own enlightenment but not as Jesus had spoken.

I can think back fifty years to the events of my fourteenth year. I hold with some clarity various moments from then. I remember what my mother and father were like. My sister, three years younger than I, holds in memory the same years with conviction similar to mine. Except she has different nuances, different memorable events, and to my horror, sometimes absolute contradictions. Memory is a tricky business. Our understanding of what Jesus said depends on the accuracy of human recollection.

When I present my father's values to my sons, his values sound like mine. To what extent have I really followed him? To what extent is it that what he said I have bent to conform to the way I want to live life irrespective of his teaching? To what extent am I selectively remembering things, removing them from context?

Jesus told us that the reign of God is like a sower going out to sow seed. Some falling on rough ground and ending up as birdseed, and some choked by weeds, and only a few seeds falling on the good soil (1).

When I hear this statement I assume that the gospel that I am reading, and the people that passed it to me, are the "good ground." Is it not just as reasonable to expect that within the community of the faithful, over the centuries, that the same proportion of fertile, weedy, and rocky ground would exist, comparable to what exists in the normal world?

Statistical theory teaches that once the number of people being studied is large enough to be a "normal" population it reacts normally. Jesus told us that we would not find his followers in the center of the bell curve where everybody is but on the edge, among the few. The king would hold a banquet, and his friends and acquaintances would be too busy to come. He would have to collect people from the streets in order to fill the hall. And they turned out to be a sorry lot indeed (2).

In the very beginning of Christianity, when the ticket to the banquet was a willingness to be fed to the lions, it was the few that were attracted. They were attracted to the table as Jesus had set it. But shortly, when Christianity became the thing to do, normal people translated the message of this abnormal man into something they found more palatable. They gathered in droves at the table but not the table as Jesus described it. They set the table they preferred.

Most Christians stopped taking Jesus seriously.

I was taught that Jesus was given to "eastern hyperbole." He did not mean it when he said the rich had a poor chance of living in the kingdom of heaven. He was just trying to shock people when he said that the dead should be left the task of burying the dead. Of course, he did not mean it when he said that I should hate my relatives. He must have meant something else. I should give of my possessions (particularly to the church) but not with the wild abandonment that Jesus suggested.

Since Christians no longer took him seriously and no longer were doing what he had asked them to do, they no longer experienced what he promised would happen to them. So they changed the message.

If they were not happy now, the happiness must come in the next life. If their daily experience of life was not changed by being a follower of the way, then the way must happen in some magical layer, deep below the surface where it cannot affect something as trivial as mood. The overwhelming spirit of God that hurled Jesus into the desert became a pale substitute called "grace" that entered the soul during Holy Communion and didn't do anything, not even feel good. The Father's love that directed his life became barely noticeable in ours.

The message of Jesus appears to be unpleasant medicine. Who wants unpleasant medicine? We are always seeking the easy way to lose weight, make money, gain strength, and look lovely. Who seeks the hard way? Yet Jesus described his way as a hard way. "Struggle to get in by the narrow door. I'm telling you, many will try to get in, but won't be able" (3).

History's solution to the Jesus problem was to remake his message to fit humankind's more natural molds. "Young wine is not poured into old wineskins, or they might break and aged wine is not poured into a new wineskin, or it might spoil" (8). His followers tried to pour his wine into some old wineskins, and the old wineskins of Judaism, Greek philosophy, and Roman organizing principles spoiled the new wine of the reign of God. Jesus' very own relatives found his message so radical that they thought he was out of his mind (Prologue). His wine had to be changed for the sake of the normal palate.

Our generation has an unusual opportunity. Half a century ago the scholars were convinced that they would never know what Jesus had really said. Now, with the addition of some newly discovered texts, and various linguistic and scientific tools, Scripture scholars are beginning to isolate the words of Jesus from those of his followers.

I offer a word of caution. It is tempting to say that they are isolating the wheat from the chaff. Not so! The words of later followers tell us much about Christianity. My favorite gospel story is the story of Jesus calming the seas. The scholars say that most likely it did not happen. Later Christians found Jesus a source of peace and they expressed that perspective in this story. So be it. My grandmother hung on her wall the picture of Jesus standing in the back of the boat, his hands lifted to calm the storm. That picture expresses perfectly her feeling, early Christianity's feeling, and my feeling that it is Jesus who has brought peace. I shall continue to hang it on my wall.

To say, "Jesus did not say it" does not remove an ancient reading from my bookshelf, or my heart. These words are important. At the same time, the Scripture scholars by winnowing out what he did not say give us a much clearer picture of who he was, and what he did say.

He was a happy man! His followers were filled with joy. They were happy because they knew something very important, something worthy of joy. If a woman loses a coin she will expend every effort to dig it out and when she finds it she will rejoice. The kingdom of heaven is like that coin worth digging for (9).

How far do we need to dig?

"God's imperial rule is right there, in your presence" (15). Jesus and his disciples have discovered a different dimension to life, and it happens right here and right now. They are living in it. They are rejoicing in it. Most people do not see it. "(God's imperial rule) will not come by watching for it. It will not be said, 'Look here it is!' or 'Look over there!' Rather, the Father's imperial rule is spread out upon the earth, and people don't see it" (15).

Could that still be true? Is the imperial rule accessible to you and I? Still?

I belonged to a ministerial association in a town in Minnesota. We instituted the practice of two ministers reading autobiographical essays summarizing their spiritual histories at each meeting. The minister of a non-denominational church read his story at one of our meetings.

He had abandoned the faith in his early teens because he was too intelligent to buy all the stuff passed on in the name of religion and he noted that nobody he knew took it seriously enough to actually invite God into his or her life to do anything. During college he became accomplished at tripping up other young people, Christian enthusiasts, for one or another stupidity.

One summer, needing a job, he signed on at a religious camp with a camp director so badly in need of staff that he ignored the fact he was adding a flaming atheist to the pot. There my friend noted some counselors given to prayer and some responses out of the ordinary run of what happens to most humans. A healing, maybe. A radical change in personality, maybe. Enough to cause him to doubt his doubt.

He faced God one evening and gave God a chance. "Now or never, enter my life or forget it." And the Divine Presence entered it. He was captured by God's loving awareness.

His chest felt like it was splitting open. Tears poured. Emotions raged ending in a feeling of deep peace and pure joy. Everything changed. If you ask him, or even if you don't, he will tell you God's reign is everywhere, but people do not see it.

One of my mainline fellow pastors missed the meeting. When I described our brother's experience to him, he said: "I knew if we kept going with this exercise we would get to the crazies eventually." As Jesus said, right here in front of them, and they don't see it.

That is one such experience. As a pastor I have heard many people tell many stories. The details vary with their religious background. Some see angels. Some simply have a feeling of transcendent peace and wholeness. One man was embarrassed as an atheist that God's presence should come to him in the shower. While I doubt that any of them would think to express their experience this way, I am certain that if I asked them if the reign of God is right here, in our presence, just an eye blink away, they would respond, "Yes."

How do we blink this eye so that we see it the way it is?

For all the stories Jesus never gave us a methodology, except to wait for the Spirit to make it all clear. Watch and pray. How do we do that? Some hints are available from the way he lived and the way he advised us to live, but as Christians we lack a procedure that causes the eye blink to occur.

This brings us to Buddhism.

The Buddha experienced enlightenment. He had a true understanding of the way things really were. He experienced happiness and felt called to teach people the insight he had received.

We humans are not that different one from another. (Our genetic maps are 98 percent the same.) Jesus and the Buddha are describing very similar experiences while living in very different cultures and therefore using quite different language, and providing different perspectives.

"Jesus was a descendent of Abraham" (Prologue). Abraham and his descendants believe that the world can be improved. It is their call from God to do precisely that. They are cocreators with God of a better universe. The Buddha lived with a circular cosmology. No getting ahead. No real change. Abraham and Jesus believed that as individuals they were responsible for their behavior. The Buddha does not even take the individual wrapping of flesh seriously. His universe is already one. The Buddhist lives in companionship with other forms of consciousness. We believe that God has given us stewardship over other forms and regard them as lesser.

The Buddha experienced compassion for all beings. We experience the Divine love pouring through us upon creation, accepting and creating in one breath.

The Buddha did not puzzle at the nature of the Divine Presence. All being one, whoever God is is already himself also. We talk to our God as someone other than us. For all of his love for the Father, so did Jesus. The great speech put on Jesus' lips saying that we are all one and should be one comes from the Gospel of John, eighty years after Jesus' death and is almost universally thought to have little to do with what the master said.

My deepest contact with the Buddha occurs in a Franciscan convent. There, I attend nine-day retreats led by various Buddhist teachers from the *vipassana* tradition. On one occasion I had stopped to solve some practical personal problem with the Franciscan nun responsible for the physical running of the house. As we parted, apropos of nothing that I remember, but perhaps to excuse this priest for sitting with Buddhists, she said: "All religions are pretty much the same."

I thoughtlessly answered "Yes" and went on to the forty-five minute meditation session. But there, the statement dogged me. Before speaking to her, I had been in the chapel sitting before

Jesus on the cross. Now I was sitting before my teachers, each reflecting the peaceful calm of the Buddha, the same calm evident in the four statues I have of him in my house. I doubt that the Buddha would have been crucified. He had no disturbing challenge to society. (Or maybe I should say that he did in that his teaching contradicted the caste system. He kept that fairly quiet.) Jesus did challenge his society, loudly, and with gestures. In that nine-day retreat I never heard the word "justice" from my teachers once. Daily my Christian prayer book prayed for it.

This is not a denigration of Buddhism. In a cosmology that knows no change, why call for change? "Live with it!" As Christians we can point to many times that our attempts to improve the universe have created questionable results. Our system is not perfect, although it is still our system.

All that aside, both Jesus and the Buddha saw the world in a way that others did not. The Buddha and his followers refined a method for creating the eye blink that makes the reign of God appear. Not infallibly. But what they created is much better than no method at all. For three thousand years they have pursued a practice of meditation that has allowed many to see the world differently. Humans being humans, rarely does a truly enlightened being emerge. But some do.

And many more come closer to understanding the Buddha's perspective.

The story is told of the Buddhist guru who was visited by westerners. One of the visitors, looking out with awe at a veritable sea of men in monastic robes, asked the guru, "How many disciples do you have?" After thought he replied: "Five . . . I think."

As Jesus said, the door is narrow, and only a few will enter. But it is there, so let us knock. For again he said that if we did knock it will be opened. If we do not knock, it probably won't be.

In the following chapters I will present the words of Jesus describing what the reign of God is like, accompanied by Buddhist techniques and insights that allow the possibility of stepping over the narrow threshold. We will take Jesus seriously. We will assume that what he offers can happen. We will learn what our fellow searchers in the East have discovered that fits with his directions.

Jesus speaks of discovering the reign of God. He offers several challenges to the blinders that are preventing us from seeing God's kingdom and experiencing God's presence. He says in effect, "Don't do it this way, do it that way, and the scales will fall from your eyes."

Buddhists have words for this. They say we live with delusions and these delusions must be seen as delusion before we can be enlightened. I will borrow their term and apply it to what Jesus has said. I will list his several challenges as challenges to the delusions that make it impossible to see the kingdom of God. I will match them up with the Buddhist challenges to the same delusions. Then we need no longer think of Jesus as using eastern hyperbole. We can take him seriously.

You will attempt to experience reality as it is without delusion, particularly that very central reality, you, yourself. When you reach that point, and it may not occur the year or decade you read this book, you will experience the Divine Presence. The Spirit of God does dwell in us. When discovered we will know that it, and it alone is the pearl of great price (9). If we discover it we will gladly sell all that we have and want nothing else.

Practical Matters

In the next chapter I will outline for you the methodology of Buddhist Insight meditation. Take some time now to discover a quiet place where you can sit for twenty minutes or half an hour without being disturbed. Find a regular time to do that. Before going on try just sitting there a couple of times. See how it feels. For now just sit five or ten minutes. Instructions come next.

If you are not going to practice meditation, reading this book makes less sense. It is like reading a book on golf while not planning to play golf or practice golf. Without swinging the club the rationale for how to grip a club will never really be learned.

Without sitting meditation much of this will sound ridiculous. Look at the instructions for a golf swing, and you will see what I mean. All the stuff about where to put body parts sounds peculiar until you try to hit a ball with them lined up differently.

Questions and Answers

1) Q: When and where did the Buddha live? Did Jesus know Buddhism?

   A: The Buddha lived centuries before Jesus and in India. I have heard from Buddhist teachers that some think that Jesus spent some time in the East and similarities in doctrine and even parables are pointed to as evidence. The Jesus scholars doubt this greatly. He is easily explainable by looking at him in his own tradition and in his own geography. If he went to the East, he didn't need to in order to know what he knew and do what he did. Some parables even have the same name. For instance, there are both Christian and Buddhist parables of the Mustard Seed. They are quite different in story and moral, however.

2) Q: How about the gods and goddesses of Buddhism? How do we deal with those?

   A: The Buddha himself had little interest in theology. The Buddha was interested in removing suffering. He accepted the historical pantheon of Buddhist gods because they were there and he was not interested in the question. In one of the discourses his disciple takes him to task for all the theological issues he has failed to address. His answer was that he had never said he was going to address those issues.

   Thomas Hand, a Jesuit priest who spent twenty-five years studying Zen in Japan as a layman (his Jesuit job was to be a language instructor,) tells this story. After six months he was allowed to see his teacher one to one. He haltingly explained to his teacher that he wanted to study

Zen but he had no intention of leaving Christianity. His teacher, who knew as little English as Father Hand knew Japanese, pointed to all the statues on the wall and said: "Buddhism." Then he pointed to the pillow Father Hand was sitting on and said: "Zen."

We are focusing on the pillow and trying to avoid the walls. This is not an easy trick because the walls are the natural container of this pillow. We are changing the container to Christianity, or at least, to "Jesusanity." Not an easy maneuver.

3) Q: Who should not take on the practice of meditation?

A: Without pursuing all things that might get in the way, I would say that people who are having trouble with their life as a human should be cautious about this. The danger is that in seeking detachment from our human desires and needs we will deny their existence or their right to exist. This balance will be difficult enough to achieve even for the healthy. Here is an example. I need to be loved, and I have been insufficiently loved as a child. In meditation practice I can try to deny my need for love. It will not work because a need is a need, but I can push myself into a dead end. Or I am unsure of my self worth. In this practice I can learn to write off "not struggling for my rights" as "denial of my ego." Again, it will not work. I will dry up as a human being.

Do not try to make your humanity go away. If this practice is getting in the way of understanding your humanity, do that first, this second. However, well used, the practice should help. You will learn that you are a conflux of forces and all you can do is work with what you got. You will learn that all thinking is anchored in a body. This is a defense against psychosis and schizophrenia. You will learn to advance the cause of your growth without fixation on goals wherever you are on the path. That insight in itself can be quite a relief.

What is sometimes experienced as emotional pain can be spiritual pain. Augustine said: "Our hearts are restless until they rest in thee, O God." Sometimes feelings of emptiness and meaninglessness can only be cured by spiritual search. So just because you feel bad is not a sign that you should not do this.

4) Q: Do Christians have parallel methods in their own tradition?

    A: I am not certain. I have not read about a Christian method of meditation that simply looks at what happens without judgment or expectation, nor one that intends to teach the attitude of detachment. However, there are many methods coming close to this such as "centering prayer." I do not know enough to discuss this. While I have read several Christian books with some hope, I have had to go this direction. It may be my limitations. I think the problem is that most Christian meditators are trapped in theological perspectives developed after the time of Jesus.

5) Q: Is the Bible fiction? Inaccurate? Accurate with some inaccuracies?

    A: To understand this you will do well to do some serious reading about the Bible, its formation, and its contents. On the subject of Jesus and the Bible, I would recommend *Meeting Jesus again for the First Time* by Marcus Borg.

    The Bible is the literature of our people, our tribe, which is a group of people called by the Spirit into following God. As literature it is all kinds of literature. Story, poetry, and history are all found in the Bible and unfortunately not always in separate books and not even in separate chapters. We have to put our experts to work telling us what verse is in which genre or even what of a particular verse is the history and what the story. The people of the day when the books of the Bible were written did not have our desire to insure that fact was separate from fiction. In a sense they anticipated modern psychology's realization that what you remember has more influence on you than what actually happened. The New Testament writers were quite content with the remembered Jesus. While I respect their approach, I want to know as much of the historical Jesus as I can.

6) Q: If the scholars say that Jesus only said or did about 20 percent of what we read on Sunday, where did the rest of it come from?

A: Scripture scholars focus on what they know, which is Scripture. Other sources tell us that most of our stories about Jesus come from the religious traditions of Greece and Rome. Pagan myths became associated with the Jesus story. Some scientists say that the function of the brain that locates us in space when confronted with the metaphysical problems of being awareness in a mortal body demands an answer. The myths give an answer. Jesus, too, had an answer to the problem. His answer was to accept the ambiguity or as he would say it, to accept the will of the Father. It is easy to understand why his early followers, and now his later ones, would find that unsatisfying. And would be eager to alter the story to give themselves more comfort.

The sad fact, however, is that the comforting answer is sugar candy compared to the bread of life. Accept the will of the Father, and you will live in the Kingdom of God now.

This is not to say that the myths are untrue. Jesus may well have risen from the dead, and you and I may very well do that too. But if you and I accept the will of the Father, we do not care. Whatever the Father wills is what will happen, and we are all right with that. As the psalm says: "Praise him for his wondrous acts."

7) Q: Why are so many of the sayings of Jesus extreme?

A: They seem extreme to us because we are extremely ignorant.

2

The Practice

Observing Delusion and Reality

Without moving
I sit at God's door
Knocking loudly.

Take Jesus Seriously

Rising early, while it was still very dark, he went outside and stole away to an isolated place, where he started to pray (5).

Explanation

I was attending family church camp. We had just sung the prayer before meals. An eight-year-old boy in front of me, perhaps desiring to impress the venerable rotund chaplain said: "In our family we pray before every meal."

I responded: "You should pray always."

What was in my head that I had to one up a little boy? I should not have done it. Congratulations to him and his family were in order. I apologize in retrospect. I heap ashes on my head in your presence.

But in the moment I could not say another word. I was flooded with a deep sensation of peace and beauty. I had accidentally uttered the eternal truth. One I had read. A truth I had never said. A truth that no one had ever said in my presence. Not even in a sermon, or a retreat lecture. One that occurred frequently in the deep spiritual books but never as a sound in my ears. Now I had said the words. I had put into a sentence my reason for life since third grade. I found myself waiting for pancakes with tears in my eyes, knowing that all would be different if I could be what I had said I should be.

At the moment I uttered this sentence the world was suddenly suffused with light, the reign of God. As I remembered God's presence, all of these mundane, camp shabby, sleepy eyed, dusty, hot people became God's angels. For a moment only and then sadly I returned.

When I say that I should pray always I do not mean a constant chatter of words to God. Words have their purpose and have their moments. Almost without fail I start my morning and end my evening with psalms and readings. I do like words; I am moved by them. Hymn singing is one of my favorite things to do. Turns me on.

However, I think of this "praying always" as my wife and I on a camping trip in the old Voyager with the pop-up, canoe, and bicycles trailing behind. We say very little. Although deeply aware of one another, fifty miles may roll by before a question, or a suggestion, or a comment. We are companions on the way. God and you and I are companions on the way.

Brother Lawrence in the *Practice of the Presence of God* says:

"I make it my business only to persevere in his holy presence, wherein I keep myself by a simple attention, and a general fond regard to God, which I may call an actual presence of God . . ."

Mother Theresa was asked what she says to God when she prays. She answered: "I say nothing, I just listen." Well then, what does God say to you? "God says nothing, God just listens." Then she added: "If you don't understand that, I can't explain it."

That is what we shall do. Become an empty vessel just listening to God with loving attention. Companions on the way.

In the Voyager I do not focus on listening to my wife. I just listen, and when my wife speaks I shall hear. So with this meditation practice, I shall just listen. My experience is that although we Christians speak of God as outside of us, what happens is that I awaken to the Divinity in me and then to the Divinity that exists in others and even things around me. This constant empty, loving, listening attitude turns the self into a playground of the Spirit and makes evident the reign of God that surrounds us.

Meditation is a practice time. It is a time to cultivate this attitude of emptiness by practicing it. We shall sit meditation as an athlete takes batting practice. He or she takes time away from the exigencies of the game to focus on one central aspect, not to become good at the practice itself, but to carry the practice into the game. The explanation for the life of Jesus, his constant attention to the will of the Father comes from the fact that "Rising early, while it was still very dark, he went outside and stole away to an isolated place, where he started to pray" (5).

I will start then my suggestions for your practice by calling to your attention that in this text he began before the day got to him. Before he was being pulled and tugged by the cares of others. These first hours frequently offer the better time to catch the mind empty, ready to listen. I have a chair in my bedroom that I use for meditation. Whenever possible my first half hour is there, still in my pajamas, unshaven, sleep snarled hair hanging, listening for the Divine Presence before the morning paper tells my mind what to think.

He said: "When you pray, go into a room by yourself and shut the door behind you" (13). From time to time I find it helpful to sit with others. There is support in seeing brothers and sisters finding their silence as I find mine. Once a year I join the Buddhists for several days and can experience the strength of the group. A Buddhist takes refuge in the Buddha, the *dharma,* and the *sangha.* The Buddha as an example of what is possible. The *dharma* is what a Christian means by "the Gospel." It is the message. The *sangha* is the community sometimes gathered. It is good to know that I am not alone.

But for this practice on a regular basis, a room by myself works much better. There is less temptation to posture for others. There are no distractions from others. I am there with whoever shows up. Gives God a better chance.

I don't pray to Jesus or even sit with Jesus. He is my elder brother. He is my example. He is my teacher. He is what God looks like when the Divine Presence glows in flesh. But he did not tell me to pray to him. The statements such as "I am the way, the truth, and the light" come not from him but later Christians. He was explicit: "When you pray, say 'Our Father, your name be revered'" (13).

So I sit in my quiet room, door shut, reminded of the presence of the Father, moving toward being an empty vessel, waiting with love, listening to whatever speaks, hoping for the Spirit and the Presence.

The practice of meditation, already refined in Buddha's day has been even more carefully studied, understood, practiced, and improved by over two thousand years of his followers. I turn to them for suggestions on what to do.

Find a comfortable position sustainable for a half-hour. Even as Jesus has been misunderstood, so has the Buddha. He said to become comfortable. His followers sat as they had sat since they were children, cross-legged on the floor. They were comfortable in that position. Now, in our time, we people who have sat in chairs since our mother stuffed us in them at age two sometimes think we are doing meditation better if we sit cross-legged, or God help us all, in the full lotus position. Then lectures and essays are given on the merits of coping with the pain. Incredible! The Buddha said to be comfortable. For most of us western Christians that means a chair. One western Buddhist guru when invited to a great international conference of top-flight practitioners was embarrassed that the easterners would see him with all of the propping pillows he used to stay erect. At the first session he was happy to note that half the old timers from India were using beach chairs.

Park your body so at least it is quiet. Inside, where the mind dwells, it is liable to be noisy. You cannot do much about that except listen. Outside you can control. Butt on a solid surface. Back straight. Stack your head right on top of your spine. You will last longer that way than if you are slouching, and you will be more comfortable. If you tip your head slightly forward so the frontal lobes are a little lower than the top of the skull it seems to quiet the mind some. Place your feet flat on the floor. Grip one thumb with the other fist, and allow the fingers of the gripped hand to rest on the back of the gripping hand. Stability will be helped if the chair is high enough that your knees are naturally lower than your pelvis. This also tilts your pelvis forward into an alert position. I add a pillow to get me at the right height. If your legs are too short to touch the floor use a pillow under your feet so that they can rest firmly. Don't sag against the back of the chair. Physical posture signals and causes internal attitude. Try for a head start on the mess inside. Have your body tell your mind to quiet down and do things in good order.

Pay attention to your breath. The mind must focus somewhere. Some practices focus on an object. Some focus on a particular thought problem. I recommend the breath, because it is always there. As long as you are alive it is available. Also, the Hindu yogis have some opinions about the breath's centrality to life and being. I am not sure how right they are, but something good happens to them by focusing on the breath. So I prefer it. Other thoughts will arise. You will find other things interesting. Perhaps even the Spirit will speak to you. So it is not the intent to pay attention to the breath at all costs or consider total centering on it the mark of successful meditation. But returning to the breath after any excursion keeps the mind centered on depth. Hopping from one thing to another leads to increased shallowness of thought and idle daydreaming. As you begin this practice of listening be strict with yourself. Back to the breath time after time until depth is achieved. Pick a particular part of the breath to focus on. Some prefer where it leaves the nose, the mustache area. Some prefer deep in the belly. A particular spot holds your focus better than a general area or sliding from place to place.

Listen with loving attention to whatever is happening in your mind. Do not try to create it. Do not become involved with it. Do not flee from it. Do not deny it.

1) Do not create it. Don't try to figure out ways to kill the time. Things will happen. You do not have to cause them. Do not even try to think pious or godly thoughts. Let what happens happen.

2) Do not become involved with it. I am thinking of my motorcycle, and I begin to think where I shall ride it, and how I shall improve it, and how I shall pay for it, and how I shall convince my wife to allow me to take a trip on it. That is involvement. When the thought first comes up, if I say to myself "daydreaming about motorcycle" or even just "daydreaming" the thought is seen, acknowledged, accepted with love, and not stuck to. Frequently I then become empty enough to rest again on my breath. This is called "labeling."

3) Do not flee from it. A sexual image sometimes arises. The temptation is to scramble for cover in horror that I who have sat to listen for the Divine Presence am experiencing a prurient image. Don't run. Look. Acknowledge. In its time it will go away. As will anything. Stay calm. This is just you. If you thought you were better than that you were mistaken. Sorry.

4) Which brings us to, don't pretend it was not there. I am often surprised at the viciousness of my planning for my "enemies" or those who have hurt me. I am vicious at times. Acknowledge it. Continue to love that which arises. The "evil" in me is not as dangerous if I know that it is there. Once I start choosing what I will listen to the odds are good I am losing my openness to God's voice.

Do not claim thoughts as yours. Do not say: "I am daydreaming." "I am breathing." "I am angry." But say: "Daydreaming." "Breathing." "Anger." You are not it. It is not you. Watching is happening. No "I" there. Be a verb. I will say more on this later. "I" implies that you are in control. Not as much as you think. Maybe you are not at all in control. The "I" to which you are referring is the boss of your personal gang of internal idiots and an idiot also. Do not name him or her in this practice. Name only the idiots with the care and love given to unruly children.

This is practice. For half an hour at a time I shall practice this attitude I hope to carry through life. Don't get too enamored with this practice. Success at it means less than developing this constant habit of listening into the rest of life. As I allow myself to become empty deep within me wiser voices speak, and I see around me the angelic depths of this created world. Daily I begin to live in the kingdom of God.

Unless you are very fortunate, graced by God in fact, little will happen very quickly. Jesus tells the story of the corrupt judge who did not want to give a widow what she deserved. So the widow just stayed on his case. The judge finally said "this widow keeps pestering me," (12) so he gave in. Sit persistently. Some of my greatest moments of deep awareness of the reign of God occurred hours after a totally discouraging half-hour spent annoyed by my devils. I pestered the Divine Presence, and God handed me a better verdict late in the day. Hang in there.

Jesus said, "Ask and it'll be given you; Seek and you'll find; knock and it'll be opened for you" (2). This practice is constant knocking day after day. Seeking month by month. Asking over the years. Keep at it. Do not allow the many times with little fruit to prevent solemnly sitting to ask again for His voice. Your love of this practice must be steadfast. It will lead you to the pearl of great price.

What then might you expect from this practice? Why do it? It is an experiment in reality. The Buddha himself begged his followers to find out for themselves what happens. Don't ask him.

To say a little, hoping to be a little helpful, and granting this might be a little harmful, let me describe what happens from time to time. I experience myself as a body. I hear thoughts, the ones running around in my head that I seldom really listen to. I become quiet and empty. I experience the nudging of the Holy Spirit with clarity. Rarely but sometimes I experience the presence of the Father as being beyond all being. Frequently in normal life, I experience reality with brightness and depth, aware living in the reign of God. I gain great pleasure from saying my prayers, particularly hymns and psalms. My focus on what is said is much sharper, and many of the great hymns and all of the psalms make perfect sense in this context. I sometimes look on my brothers and sisters with love and compassion provoked only by who they are and what they face. I experience the divine love flowing through me to all of being.

Why wouldn't Buddhists describe the same thing? In a sense, they would. What is happening is that I am having experiences opened to me by the practice of meditation. I already have in my head a map of how the universe works passed on to me by my religious heritage as does my Buddhist friend. The words "reign of God" spring to my lips, when "enlightenment" would spring to hers. I think a Navajo might say, "Hozra," which is the word for the beauty that they walk in when they walk in beauty. Same experience, I think. They are using a different map.

As I have said before, I prefer my map. I think it more accurate. I find it slightly clumsy for this form of meditation but much better for understanding work, and play, and sex and how to have a rousing worship service. But then, why would I not? It's my map. Ingrained from childhood.

I am not saying that reality is relative. Reality is reality. The maps, however, are indeed relative.

The Buddha did not worry about theology. He said that if a man has been shot with an arrow in the chest and comes to a surgeon, the surgeon removes the arrow without conversation about who might have shot it. The Buddha accepted his era's theologians for their picture of the divine. Then he sat and listened to remove the arrow of suffering. I accept with joy and pleasure my Christian cosmology. I think it correct enough granted the difficulty of doing better. And then I sit quietly, listen, try to be empty, and see what comes. I wait with love but without expectation. Yet, I know that the experience of the depths will probably come to me in the categories my mother gave me, at least at first.

Basic Points to Remember about Practice
- Pick a time or times when the mind is not crowded by what has happened or is about to happen.
- Find a quiet spot and close the door.
- Sit comfortably, back straight, head tilted slightly forward, butt solid, and knees below pelvis. No slouching for back support.

- Focus on the breath for depth. When in doubt return to the breath. Focus on the breath in a specific spot in your body.
- Allow thoughts and feelings to come. Observe them with love and acceptance. Without panic name them. When they go away return to the breath. Do not even identify the thought as yours. No "I" in this, just "watching." Be a verb.
- Do not make this an end in itself. It is an attitude you shall try to bring into life. There is no such thing as being good or bad at meditation. It is what it is.

Persist. This is hard. Demanding. Persist.

> *Quietly sitting*
> *Waiting with love for*
> *Whatever comes?*

Questions and Answers

1) Q: What should I do with my eyes?

   A: There are many alternatives used by various practitioners ranging from eyes wide open to eyes completely shut. The alternative I am most comfortable with is to look down at about a forty-five degree angle at the floor in front of me and keep the eyes unfocused and partially open. You will create rather a blurry vision of just the floor. On occasion I look around at things to note what is pleasant to see and what unpleasant, and on occasion I close my eyes completely. I find that when sitting in a circle with fellow students my eyes tend to close more often. When in a forward facing group, they are more likely to be open.

2) Q: I cannot shut out noises. They keep attracting my attention.

   A: A noise is a sound that you have decided not to like. Don't judge sounds. Let them be. Treat them as anything else that is crossing your mind. The only difference between them and a thought or feeling is that they were instigated by stimuli of the skull. Try to notice the way they vibrate in your ear. Label them and gradually they will lose their interest for you and you will return to the breath. If they are so intense and constant that you cannot treat them with placid indifference and loving attention you may simply be in a poor place for you to meditate. Move.

3) Q: You are quite insistent on starting on time. Is there any reason for this other than compulsiveness?

   A: Yes. We want to arrive at the point where our consciousness has dominance over our bodies and our environment. When we start late it is because we have allowed the environment and its demands to have precedence over our conscious intention. If the only reason we are on time is compulsiveness, then we are giving in to a nervous disorder, which is as far off the mark as giving in to the environment. These are both ways of declaring ourselves asleep.

4) Q: Sometimes songs stick in my head and will not go away no matter how hard I try.

   A: Anything you struggle with tends to struggle back. Force is met by counterforce. Learn not to struggle. Watch it. Label it as "singing." Focus on the label not the singing. Wait for it to come to its own completion. Lots of life would leave us more peacefully if we did not struggle with it.

5) Q: What does it mean to be in relationship to God?

   A: I presume that you are having difficulty experiencing yourself in relationship to God. I suspect that the problem is that to be in relationship you have to be in relationship with someone or something outside of yourself. Since the Divine permeates all things, and seeing the kingdom of God is to see the Divine, I cannot be in relationship to the Divine, I can only experience the Divine. To take this even further, I cannot, as I live in the kingdom, even experience something other than myself as completely other since it too is permeated with the Divine. Which brings us to the Buddhist formula of non-dualism, thou and I are not two, although we are not one either.

To experience oneself in relationship to God what one does is crystallize part of the experience of the Divine and project it as if it were a person and then interact with it. Numbers of people have done this quite successfully, and for some this is the easy way. For others, apparently you, it may be easier to be aware of the experience of divinity in self and others.

That is certainly the direction this practice moves a person. Since I am Christian and raised a dualist, in this book I will often speak of God as someone completely separate. The bureaucrats who do not have a sense of the underlying unity have dominated the Christian tradition. The mystics who have only a weak sense of duality have dominated the Buddhist tradition. Sometimes I will speak from one perspective. Sometimes from the other.

6)   Q: I have taken meditation practice before, and I was told to focus on a candle flame and ignore everything else. I found this pleasant. It helped me be peaceful. Why am I being told to pay attention to distractions?

A: There are two types of meditation. One seeks peace and the other seeks understanding. Both have their value. The type you used to take helps you forget what is going on in ordinary life. It is a vacation. It is refreshing. The down side is that ordinary life does not change as a result of it.

The type of meditation I am teaching seeks to understand what is happening. The focus is to be deeply aware of reality. Doing this can change ordinary life into extraordinary life. You can wake up to the kingdom of God. The downside is that frequently it is very annoying, sometimes downright painful. In one of my deepest moments of meditation in a large group somebody had to tell me to be quiet because I was disturbing people. As I recall I was wrestling with three distractions and desperately wanted to return to my breath, and I felt as if my mind was about to disintegrate from the strain. I did not have much fun, but at least one of the causes of my suffering in life died that very day.

If you want to impress your friends, tell them that the meditation seeking peace is called *suka* meditation for "sweet," and our kind is called *duka* meditation or suffering meditation because we are pursuing what makes us suffer so that we can stop suffering.

7) Q: What are the numbers after the Jesus quotes?

A: They refer to the chapter they are taken from in *The Gospel of Jesus according to the Jesus Seminar.*

—

I, who live by words, am wordless when
I try my words in prayer. All
language turns
To silence. Prayer will take my words
and then
Reveal their emptiness. The stifled voice learns
To hold its peace, to listen with the heart
To silence that is joy, is adoration.

Madeleine L'Engle

—

3

Replacing Delusions
with Material Reality

Sitting
I await the Divine Presence
patiently.

Take Jesus Seriously

Whoever does not accept God's imperial rule the way a child
would, certainly won't set foot in God's domain (2).

Explanation

Before emptying ourselves, we need to begin the process of
emptying material reality of ourselves. Some people are never in
contact with the physical world. Most people are seldom in contact with reality irrespective of themselves. They project their
own reality onto God's flowers and then cannot see anything but
themselves mirrored on the petals of the rose.

Driving fast or shooting rapids or bungee jumping wakes us
to material reality. Life becomes bright for a while, but then it
dulls and another thrill is needed. Buying a new car awakes the
pleasure of driving. But this lasts only for a while.

What is going on?

When I was a child and a bird landed on a tree limb, I was
awestruck at the reality of this flying colored thing. My mother
explained to me that that was a "bird." It took a while but even-

tually I learned to say "bird" when one of those bursts of color arrived. Indeed, now the bird lost its glamor. I knew what it was. It was this name "bird." I no longer even had to look at it. "Bird" was on the back porch. With time, I no longer saw birds at all. The stimulus of one of those objects awakened in my head a concept called "bird." I had substituted noticing the concept in me for paying attention to the object out there. I no longer saw the flower but I saw my idea of a flower mirrored on the petals of the rose. I learned to live with the delusion that I saw.

I will use the word "delusion" often from now on and in several contexts. By it I always mean a concept that you and I have created that we see instead of the reality that is there. Indeed some concepts such as "success" or "riches" or "future" are created out of such flimsy material that one might almost say that there is no reality there.

I grant that "delusion" is a painful word. I know that from the response of groups that I have taught who have poured upon me rage that I would suggest that they might be deluded. The word "delusion" implies a responsibility for the creation of the unreal that no one wants to assume. But, granting the complicity of society, who else creates my delusions, if not me?

There is merit in this process of creating concepts and delusions. If it did not occur I would still be on the back porch going "oh" and "ah" whenever a bird arrived. I would inch down the front walk moving from rose to petunia to pansy. A yard full of dandelions might stop me for a day. As it is I can walk to the car expeditiously and drive to work. This is a useful endeavor in a normal life.

When psychedelic drugs don't blow the mind completely, they have this delightful effect of momentarily removing the delusion and allowing a person to see reality. This is a risky business of course. Timothy Leary, the psychedelic guru, responded to the accusation that he was trying to avoid reality by saying that those skipping drugs were avoiding reality. Indeed we are. We prefer having concepts stand between reality and us to using mind-blowing drugs. Most of us do not want to take a chance that we will be allowed pure reality in one moment but later need someone to feed us our oatmeal.

We can have this direct look at reality absent delusion without drugs. Children do it all the time. I have a picture of my son at age four living in pure reality without delusion. He is captured by one of those department store photos. My wife took the boy to the second floor of Sears, and just as the picture was snapped Ben spied a huge bubble, as big as a basketball, that had floated up the steps from some event on the first floor. It is clear that he is not saying "bubble." No concept there. No delusion. Awe and joy at this marvelous thing radiates from his face. Wonder!

Jesus said: "Whoever does not accept God's imperial rule the way a child would, certainly won't set foot in God's domain" (2).

This is the reason that Jesus had a bias for children. It is not that they are so innocent, although some are. Not that they are so kind. Lord knows many are not kind at all. It is not that they do good. Even the best of them doesn't do much to improve the earth. But they see the world that is there. They experience it directly and not through some intermediary idea.

I once woke to a flat indecipherable scene of grays, browns, greens, and a little blue. This lasted but a bare second. Then in rapid order I realized I was in the front seat of the Voyager, that I must be looking at the St. Olaf College campus, that I was seeing a gray stone fence, before a brown building surrounded by green grass, bushes and trees and a little blue sky peeking through the foliage.

I had read in my college psychology texts that I create the order that I think I see, but this, and two other such instances, dramatically demonstrated that without my ordering mind, I could not rely on my eyes to show me a building.

In the Gospels, when the blind man of Bethsaida was healed, he said: "I see human figures as though they were trees walking around"(16). In one version Jesus had to try the healing process again to assure that newly cured person's mind made better order out of what it was seeing. Several times when living in deep peace I too have seen human figures as if they were trees walking. Removed of preconception of what we look like, walking trees are what we look like. At least this is the way we appear to me. Take my word for it.

My wife attended an art camp. To be a good scout I went along, and since they would not let me just be there I signed up for landscape painting. To me the art instructor usually said something like: "Will you just *look* at the goddam stick (or lake, or canoe, or hill, or house.) You are painting what you think is there. If you will just see what is there, it will go much better."

I finished by creating two paintings that I am pleased with, not proud, but content. I will never be a painter, but for one week I gradually learned to see what was in front of me and at least know when I was not seeing it. Because when I saw it, it glowed. Everything. Whatever. It glowed. William Blake, the English poet and artist, saw a reality others thought a little strange. Brightness. I think that nearly is what I saw, when I saw. If the colors are not bright, I now know, I am asleep.

Sounds arise while meditating. Out there somewhere vibrations are created in the air. These vibrations reach through to us. The old philosophical question if a tree falls in the forest without a human around, is there a sound? The answer is "no." For sounds are what a human makes out of disturbances in the air.

> To study the Buddha-way is to study the self.
> To study the self is to forget the self.
> To forget the self is to be enlightened by the ten thousand things.
>
> That the self advances and confirms the ten thousand things is called delusion.
> That the ten thousand things advance and confirm the self is enlightenment.
>
> —Dogen Zenji, the thirteenth century Japanese Zen master who brought Soto Zen from China to Japan.

"The ten thousand things" refers to all reality that is out there. If you can forget yourself they will appear in your awareness as they are, and you will be enlightened. If you try to make them in your image, you will deal not with the ten thousand things but with your own delusions. If you let them enter you, you will understand your true nature, which you share with them and will experience enlightenment.

Jesus was referring to this phenomenon when he talked about seeing the reign of God as children do. This is not his total message of course. But this manner of paying attention as a child does, bare of any judgment or even concept, is the first step in facing on a gut level the existential questions. The Divine Presence appears in the child's world in response to the question that surges from the shock of seeing bare reality without the cushion of concept: "How can this be?"

Reality seen creates wonder. Any reality seen will create wonder. True seeing wakes us to the fact that we see. We are. Wonder asks how this can be. The Divine Presence arrives in answer.

So what if I see as a child sees? What difference will it make if I reduce the times I see concepts and not reality? Other than psychedelic glows, that is. Having had a few such glows, I will say that they are enough for me, but they are not all that is.

I was a consultant to the Senior Vice-President for Research and Development at a huge corporation. He was a Ph.D. in some esoteric form of mathematics. His office was the size of a large living room and his desk an oaken masterpiece. His chair was a veritable leather throne. Commenting on a colleague of mine one day, he said: "I appreciate Dick. He always makes me feel comfortable."

Why would such a man need to be made comfortable? I, until that moment, had never really looked at the man himself. I had been interacting with the titles, the desk, the chair, and the room, all of which had created in me the concept of a powerful, secure, overwhelming presence of a man. With clean eyes, I saw he who was there. He had a bright intellect, but poor social skills. Discomfort with other people. Hiding in work. He was not even trying to conceal who he was. I just had never looked. Because I had never looked I had never cared for the real person who was there. I had danced with delusions.

When a child learns to say "mommy," the real mommy begins to disappear. Now instead of flesh and blood, wants and needs, strengths and weakness, a concept intervenes of a superwoman able to do all things. The "unexpected" is replaced with the "for sure." But the "for sure" is a delusion. Have you had the experience somewhere in your twenties perhaps of waking up to your real parent, the human being beyond your concept? Is it not wonderful? And frightening. She even dies. For that reason can you not feel your heart surge toward this actual person in a manner the concept never provoked?

This will be one aspect of your meditation practice, to learn what is your concept and distinguish it from what is really there. Leave the land of delusion for the land of reality. Replace chimeras with that which can be loved. Enter the world of wonder where we shall see the reign of God spread before us.

We begin with what we feel as we sit, for we are material reality also. There are four objects of Buddhist meditation practice: body, feeling, mental contents, and state of mind. Our basic estrangement from ourselves is our forgetfulness that the last three, feeling, mental contents, and state of mind are happening in the first. If we can come aware of the fact that we are awareness in a body, all else will make sense. For this reason the masters harp on body awareness and awareness of the rest of material reality as it presents itself to our senses. Even when I am aware of a feeling or a thought or an emotional state, I need to be aware of it as it exists in the body.

So we begin with what we feel as we sit.

Some quite physical facts will emerge after a few minutes. Perhaps the bottom will begin to get sore. Perhaps the back will begin to hurt. Maybe the nose itches. Mine is quite prominent and often itches grandly. So for an example let us settle on this often-explored (by me) itching proboscis.

There is the itching, and there is the concept of the itching. The concept is that an unbearable insult is being inflicted on my anatomy that requires immediate attention. The reality is considerably less difficult. The thing just itches. So let me pay attention to it. Allow it to come to the foreground. Stop trying to not pay attention to it and focus on it. Not the concept now. But the itching. Usually I discover I'm not suffering at all. I am just itching, and the itching goes away.

If it does not go away, then I practice deliberately doing something about it, but without desperation and only after exploration. Slowly bring my hand up and gently scratch the minimum number of times to make it go away.

This is not about winning and losing. It is about awareness. If I scratch the itch immediately, I do it with minimal awareness. If I observe the itch first without scratching, then I can also observe the desire to scratch before I make a move. I can observe the desire not to scratch, and then I can observe the move itself. I identify neither with the itch or the desire to scratch or the desire not to scratch or the scratch, so which ever dominates I don't win. I watch.

Do the same for pain, or even pleasure. A smell that I like distracts me from the breath. No panic. What is it? where is it happening? Delight in it. It will shift into the background in time, and if it does not at least the meditation period passed pleasantly.

Jesus continually told us not to worry. The worry begins here. We have a reality that may be difficult, but then we add a concept to it, and it becomes terrible. As a consultant it becomes evident that one of my clients no longer wants me. I now have empty time coming. But no, I know that "empty time" is below standard for a great consultant. I add the concept "failure" to the pot. While I am at it, I add another concept, "harbinger of further failure." Sweat breaks out at the possibility that my whole life shall change in terrible ways. "Terrible ways" is my concept to put on ordinary work instead of the incredible opportunities I have now, ordinary pay instead of the fat paychecks I bring home presently. Just as I poured my concepts on the reality of a bird with my judgments and concepts, I now reshape the flower of empty time with my images and then no longer see empty time in itself but as the mirror of my own images. I am deluded, and I assure you, I, and no one else, am responsible.

But what should I do about something really serious? I have a pain in the belly. I see the doctor. He tells me I have cancer. My life is ruined. Is it ruined because of the physical fact? Not really. The pain is still whatever it was and may be so for months or years. The end is just as likely as it was before the diagnosis. The prognosis is whatever it is. But the concept "cancer" is life ruining. I can no longer be happy. I have cancer. I cannot listen to a bird sing. I cannot hug a child. I cannot ride a motorcycle. I must sit and brood, now that I have the big "C."

I have no right to cite my own experience on this because I have not yet faced anything this grave personally. Others have. The AIDS community reports many people who decided to make their disease no bigger than it was and entered radiant lives. Joy beyond joy. For some for the first time they experienced life itself and escaped all other concepts as they accepted coming death and just lived the daily experience. They said: "I am not dying with AIDS; I am living with AIDS." And then they created a community of love that put the churches to shame.

I have a friend who likes driving a school bus as a job because it gives him the privilege of spending the middle of the day with his wonderful twenty-five-year-old son. They will bicycle together, visit parks, and do small projects. In winter they will cross-country ski. His son is available because he has the mental age of an eight-year-old. Just think how my friend could waste his life by cursing fate that God gave him a child that does not fit the concept. He does not waste a minute, because he sees the child God did give. More than wonder enough. He has been given a fitting person to receive his love.

Fearlessness is required here. That is what prevents us from allowing the reality to emerge. We are afraid of the real, so we would substitute the concept. We are afraid of the itch as it is, so we invent delusions about it that are much more frightening than the itch that is there. We are afraid of the cancer as it is, so we invent a much worse delusion of what is happening than what is there.

UU (THE BOTTOM LINE)

We are taking seriously Jesus saying: "Whoever does not accept God's imperial rule the way a child would, certainly won't set foot in God's domain" (2). What are we doing with our bodies? Through half open eyes we are seeing whatever we see and hearing with quiet ears whatever we hear. Experiencing in our bodies whatever is going on. Feeling our breath where it is at, as it is there and not as we think it might be. All of this that when we walk out the door we shall see the tree as it is, the walkway as it is, the flowers as they are, the hum of the car's motor as it is, the person across the lunch table as she is, and the cup of tea that is there. Without judgment the real calls for our love as it is. We are being little children.

Loving attention!

Then, because it is God's domain and because our eyes are now the non-judgmental eyes of a child, we shall see the glory that is there. As the Navajo sings, we shall walk in beauty. Before us, above us, beside us, below us, behind us.

In itself, this is enlightenment. If you could simply sit in meditation and simply be aware of your breath, or anything for that matter, with loving attention, absent delusion, you would experience the unity of all things in the Divine Presence, your heart would be absorbed in love.

Practical Matters

Are you paying attention to the breath? Most people cannot just focus on the breath for the entire sitting period, but if you find that you leap from thought to thought and never come back to the breath, it is very likely that you are moving at an increasingly shallow level, not really paying attention to anything. Come back to the breath whenever you can. Focus on a specific aspect of the breath. Some like the mustache area, as the breath leaves the nostrils. Some prefer the very bottom of the stomach. But pick a spot and keep coming back to that spot.

We are awareness in a body. If, as most people do, you find yourself floating from thought to thought you are literally crazy, you are not floating. All this is happening in your body. Come back from crazy land. Live where you really are. Become like a little child who has not learned to float in the crazy land of concepts

Questions and Answers

1) Q: When I sit I often lose the sensation of my body being there and experience just the head and sometimes not even that.

   A: I believe what you are experiencing is called "sinking mind." If you wish to recover from it, simply move your body slightly. What is happening is that in the absence of kinetic feedback the mind loses its awareness of the body. The form of meditation I am teaching encourages awareness. Don't float. It is not real.

2) Q: I would like to use a timer or a tape to time the length of my sitting so I need not be concerned about how much time is spent and how much left.

   A: Well sure. But. Watch out for the mad disease of the meditation shopper. There are catalogs full of stuff that you could buy to assist you in meditation. Then this practice starts to become a thing in itself, filled with precious feelings of mastery. The point of all this is to make it possible for you to sit in your office and experience what is around you, and experience the Divine Presence at the same time. Looking at a watch is not counterproductive. "I am aware of my concern about the time. It does not go away as I am aware of it. I am aware of looking at my watch to alleviate my concern about time." Bingo. It's fixed. You will have to do that when you are sitting in your office. Can you remember the Divine Presence while changing a diaper? That is the direction we are headed.

3) Q: What is a zafu? What is a zabuton?

A: A zafu is a hard round pillow used as a seat for those sitting cross legged or in a lotus position. The zabuton is the mat under the pillow to protect the legs and whatever. They tell me that if you can meditate that way you will be better grounded. I doubt it. My friend, Dosho Port, head teacher at Clouds in the Water Zen Center, insists from his own experience that this is true. I still doubt it.

4) Q: Why label in meditation, when the encouragement was to see what is there as a child sees it, which would be without even concept, certainly without label?

A: The intent is not to get stuck in some phenomena. So when phenomena arise, they are to be noticed as a child notices, without concept. But if they continue sticking in the mind, in order to move on, label them. They will become uninteresting, you can return to the breath, and the next thing will have room to come up. Eventually, when everything that is there normally has been noticed the mind will become quieter.

5) Q: Is reality always better than the world the mind creates? Doesn't the mind sometimes protect an individual from something that is extremely painful?

A: You are absolutely correct. In that case it is not wise to force through the protections, unless with trained psychological help. A trained psychologist would be cautious about shredding delusions. However, even then, it would be better if the painfulness went away and the individual could look at the world as it is instead of as it seems. Such is the goal of some kinds of therapy. (I suspect the goal of most therapy is to allow a person to survive in this world as it defines itself.) This practice, watching without interfering, tends to help by uncovering what it uncovers at a speed the mind can tolerate. Sometimes, but rarely, it moves too fast, and therapy is required.

T. S. Eliot in *The Cocktail Party* has his heroine, Celia, go to a psychiatrist because she cannot fit into normal life. A wise man, he begins by saying that before helping her become normal he must learn what normal is for her. Her problem turns out to be that she is living in the kingdom of God and cannot understand normal deceits.

The interaction between psychology and seeking is subtle. For some people it is enough that they learn to live with their delusions. Others cannot tolerate such a life and must undertake the spiritual journey.

6) Q: How can I pray in tune with this practice? Saying words seems out of place.

A: The prayer I recommend is simply holding the object of the prayer in love. In a sense that is what we do when we meditate. Everything that comes up receives our loving awareness. We wish neither that it change nor that it improve but we love it as is and wherever it goes. A slight extension of that is to deliberately, insofar as we can deliberately do anything, bring a person or a situation into loving attention and wish it well. I breathe in, and I call Jean's name and face into my loving attention, and as I breathe out, I wish her well. I don't call on God in this practice because I know that the Spirit dwells in me, and if I wish her well so does the Divine Presence. Perhaps even better, the Divine always wished her well; I am providing a voice for its intentions. In the process I become even more aware of the Divine in me as divine love arises in me provoked by the rising of her face into my awareness.

As I say, this is meditation with a touch more direct-edness. Something very like this in the *vipassana* tradition is called *metta* meditation.

7)   Q: Sometimes I feel trapped in my body. Claustrophobic. What can I do?

A: Since you are the only one in there, it must be you that is confining you. Give yourself permission to wiggle when you feel claustrophobic. Most likely the permission itself will fix it. If it does not, then wiggle, or stand, or walk. Suffering is not the point. Awareness is the point.

8)   Q: I want to check something out. I am going through a fairly anxious and painful time right now. What I am finding about the sitting is this: When fear or anxiety comes up and I acknowledge it and name it without iden-tifying with it, it calms down so fast I'm suspicious. Can all these feelings I've carried for so many years be that easy to deal with? Of course they come up again later, but I am finding that the sitting is indeed "practice" and that I can concentrate on my breathing, name the feeling, and it dissipates even when I am not sitting. Will doing this repeatedly help me build a center not run by my fears? Without unhealthily repressing them? It seems promising, but I wanted to check it out. I know you are not a psychologist, but what is your experience, opinion?

A: You are the best judge of what happens to you. You are very aware of your fears normally and that awareness causes you difficulty. Most of us are very fearful but un-aware of our fears because we move to avoid them before we are conscious of them. We lead leaden lives to avoid awareness of fear. In that context, I rejoice that you are able to be aware of them and that they dissipate. I cannot tell you if this is the beginning of life without fear or not. You will find out over time. Some live without fear, and it is a life of extraordinary brightness.

At least, I see no reason why you would become less skillful at this practice than you find yourself now. If it works now it should work forever. But over time, you will know. I might caution that you avoid thinking it is magic. It is a skill. Sometimes great basketball players go through a scoring slump because they think they were able to hit shots because of magic and begin throwing the ball in the general direction of the hoop. They have to remember it is a skill and concentrate on what they are doing. As will you.

I am happy for you. I pray this continues for you.

9) Q: Since this is a spiritual practice I assume that we are trying to live beyond the world of sensations and become
pure awareness. Is that the direction?

   A: Wrong on several counts. I suggest that "trying" will get
you nowhere. Don't try. Just sit and see what happens.
We do want to be aware, but not "pure awareness" since
the body is really there, and it is far from pure. And practiced rightly we become very sensitive to sensations, that
is what impure awareness is like. While sitting we reduce
the number of sensations in the room to make it easier to
notice those sensations that remain. And outside of the
moment of practice, we focus on sensations as they arise
in our walking through life.

Much of our society attempts to experience sensation by drowning in them. A chocolate fudge sundae is an
example of drowning in sensation, and quite probably
not feeling much because the senses are overwhelmed. A
single cup of tea and a cookie would be more fitting to
one who practices. Every bite, and every sip noticed, and
the feel of the chair and the placement of the dishes, and
their color. All pulled into awareness.

4

Escaping the Delusion that We Are Our Feelings and Thoughts

My mind
Balloon floating free
Watches.

Take Jesus Seriously

Whoever does not accept God's imperial rule the way a child would, certainly won't set foot in God's domain (2).

Explanation

Now that we have explored what it is like without preconception to turn a calm gaze at the material world, our body and what it senses, are we willing to turn that same calm, loving gaze on feelings and thoughts? Not to analyze or judge, just to look.

The answer for most of us raised in the Christian tradition is "No way!"

We are willing to look, but we are not willing to look *calmly*. That we have control over our own thoughts and feelings is an earthshaking Christian error creating its tremors from the hearts of prurient teenagers to the beleaguered souls of the dying. One of my friends discovered her first-grade son praying to be delivered from his impure thoughts.

We think we are our feelings and thoughts. Because we have responsibility we cannot simply see what is there. We either see what we hope is there, or we see what is there with judgment, sometimes pleased as punch but much more likely wishing we were better. You and I have been trained in this, and this will be hard to shake. To simply love what is there absent judgment. Love it without comparing it to a standard of what is right or wrong.

The process of gazing at our thoughts and feelings as taught here has no basis in Christian teaching that I know. Christians have always thumped themselves for thoughts and feelings. The Desert Fathers (and Mothers I suppose) beat themselves bloody, literally, to prevent certain thoughts and feelings. Therefore they had more of them, and hallucinations as well.

Wells and springs will clean themselves if allowed to run. The mind and heart will clean themselves if you can look at them calmly. Block the stream and it gets dirty, cloudy, and foul. This is a simple fact. Modern psychology knows this. The Buddhist knows this. Jesus did not say otherwise. The scholars tell us that the words attributed to him about sins of the heart were concocted by a later Christian.

Thoughts and feelings run through us. They are caused by external events past and present interacting with our bodily structures. We don't control them, and they are not us. We can watch them.

I call this loving attention. There are six characteristics of this attention:

1. *Evenly Suspended:* I am not trying to pay attention to a specific thing. I am just paying attention. Image the conscious awareness as a helium balloon floating in space. Put eyeballs on one side of it, but do not see the eyeballs focused on anything. Watch the balloon float up or down or sideways with small eddies of air. The eyeballs simply rotate whenever the balloon rotates. Put a gentle smile on its face. Whatever it sees it smiles upon not that it judges anything good,

it simply accepts and loves everything as it is. Just watch this balloon in your imagination for a little bit, please. It is without intention. Just floating. Going nowhere. Nowhere to go. In meditation you are floating on the breath, out and in.

2. *Openness:* Now, in the proximity of this balloon, something of interest arises. The eyes seek to focus. No turning away, no ignoring. The balloon slowly rotates to allow the eyes to look. Not the swift penetrating alert turning of the hawk towards prey, but this contented balloon more and more drawn to whatever has moved close to its view. In meditation, a thought of my motorcycle, a feeling of joy in its power, a picture of it in splendid redness, and then enough, I shall again float back to my breath.

3. *Fearlessness:* See again the balloon. From behind comes a snarl, a tiny man with a big pin. Does the balloon close its eyes? Not at all, just as before it slowly arcs and turns focusing on the danger. Studying it without fear. Loving attention even to a threat. In meditation, being lovingly aware of hatred, rage. Attention turns, explores, sees what has been hurt, loses interest, and returns to the breath.

4. *Astonishment:* Being astonished does not depend on you. Seeing infinity in a grain of sand will frequently knock you onto your back. Reality is indeed God's kingdom. If you can look at it for only a moment you will be astonished. One of my teachers had to sit on the bumper of some stranger's car while she recovered from an accidental moment of loving attention while walking through a supermarket parking lot. Even in a supermarket parking lot, the kingdom of God is a lot to handle.

5. *Impersonality:* Do not take on these feelings and thoughts as yours. They come into attention out of nowhere. They disappear into nowhere. They momentarily exist in your

awareness. They are most certainly not yours. You are most certainly not they. Thousands of forces have created them, from your father's grumping, to the skinny woman on TV wearing hardly any clothes, to the potato digesting in your intestines, to your mother's desire that everything happen neatly. You are just watching the result of all that. Be a verb. Be "watching."

6. *Transitional Space:* You are a momentary space through which things pass. Nothing stays. All simply rolls in, on and outward. You do not expect things to stay in your mind. When they enter you await their passage. You are just a space. As you observe you will discover that much of who you think you are is a delusion. It is not you. It is just passing through. Be a verb.

This is the way to live life. No clinging to the pleasant and no avoiding the negative. Just letting whatever come and go. Be a verb. Be "watching."

Is this not like Jesus? I see him living this way. "Why did he say that then?" The answer seldom if ever is that it made strategic sense to say that then. The most obvious answer is: "Because that is what came up." Peter is anointed as the rock on which Jesus will build, and then he is the Satan who is to get out of Jesus sight. Jesus is not thinking this out. In Christian language it is "Living at the behest of the Spirit."

If you will accept this attitude during meditation, you may be surprised to see how much room exists inside your body and head. The balloon floats in a vast space. Thoughts and feeling move into its context, appearing first in the distance, disappearing after a time into a universal space.

Oh, wow.

The scientists of the brain have discovered that we have not one brain but three. We begin with the brain of the reptile, add on to it the brain of the mammal, and then stick on top that most unusual development, the brain of the human. All three are tightly interwoven. What affects one tends to affect the others.

What we do in meditation is allow the brain of the human to observe the reptile and mammal brains as they go about their business of running our lives. We do not regret these grasping, greedy, lusting, scheming little things. Without them we would be dead ten thousand times over by now. We need their desperate efforts to find shelter, food, sexual intimacy, safety, insurance, and all that they do. We need their efforts, but we need not ourselves become desperate. This human brain floating as a helium balloon simply watches, observes. We identify with the human brain, and observe the others.

Nearly half a century ago Carl Rogers noticed the immense curative powers of acceptance. His form of therapy involved the therapist simply reflecting back to the client the feelings and thoughts the client had just stated in a form that indicated that the therapist accepted these feelings and thoughts as they were. She did not judge, not necessarily agreeing but granting the absolute right to the client to have these thoughts and feelings. There was no negative judgment, no positive judgment. The client's illness is rooted in not being willing to accept his or her own feelings and thoughts. As these feelings and thoughts are accepted, the client is able to move beyond them.

In the many times that I will refer to "being aware," and "paying attention," and "accepting" this is the thought and feeling I am referring to. The Japanese word for "mind" also denotes what we in English would refer to as heart. This "acceptance" is not cold blooded. This "awareness" is suffused with love for its object irrespective of the object changing or staying the same. This "attention" is openness not only of the mind but also of the heart. So I will use an adjective with a noun such as "loving attention," or "loving awareness" where a *vipassana* teacher might say "bare attention."

As our helium balloon projects its gentle acceptance upon the processes of the mammalian and reptilian brain, life quiets down and improves. A little like the warmth of the sun descending into a frozen and frightened land.

I use the words "acceptance/detachment" together often. The acceptance given here is not one that clings to the reality of what it sees. The person simply sees the reality, knowing full well that all is transitory. If what he sees is painful, it will pass. If what she sees is pleasant, it too will pass. The soul remains detached from these objects neither pushing away the painful or holding on to the pleasant. The detachment is a quality of the acceptance. The acceptance is a quality of the detachment.

A pleasant exercise, one that puts this process in front of you where it can be seen, is to take pen to paper for fifteen minutes and simply write whatever comes to mind. Let it flow. It becomes a meditation on paper. Do not rush the pen frantically, but on the other hand do not ever let the pen stop. If confused, write: "I am confused." If bored, write: "I am bored."

Back now to the practice. As thoughts and feelings arise observe them with quiet acceptance and detachment. If the observation begins to get sticky, you begin to get hooked, your mind begins to race, label the thought or feeling. Put a name on it. "Planning," "thinking," "daydreaming," "lusting." Let it know you know it is there. Like a child, it wants your attention. It needs your love. Give it or it screams louder.

Check out where it lives in the body. Thoughts and feelings are not things happening in some spirit world, they are experiences within our bodies.

Some psychologists say that the psychological unconscious is buried there, in the neurons, cells, and blood stream. The psychic is physical. As we observe our body, we observe our mind. As we observe our mind, we observe our body. Where else would the unconscious be? Would it be in a bag up in the air? Floating is crazy. It's all in the body.

See where the anger is running. Heart beat quicker? Where does the fear live? My fear lives in the middle of my belly. Thinking runs around in my head. Anxiety lives in my neck and shoulders. Instead of just saying "anxiety" say also: "Tension in my neck and shoulders." Focus there. As well as naming the fear, find the butterflies in the belly. Focus there. Look at them where they live, and then they move on. All is transitory.

If they don't move on, my experience is that I have mislabeled them. I have such faith in the label. Normally, it raises a wall against further thinking. Some things I nearly always mislabel. For instance "anger," is usually really "hurt." I can say "anger" ten times and remain repeating the thoughts. If I say "hurt" once and watch the ache down by my heart, peace will descend. (Anger is a reaction to hurt.)

"Jesus used to say: 'Be passersby'" (3). This is the way I look at my thoughts and feelings. It is as if I was walking by a stadium and, hearing the shouts of the crowd, I entered to see two teams playing soccer. I have no allegiance to one over the other. I am a passerby. I just watch with love and pleasure in what is happening and no interest in the outcome.

One Buddhist teacher when asked if he still struggled with his meditation practice after years and years of sitting on the pillow said: "Oh no, I just sit down and say to myself, 'Let the show begin.' Whatever comes up is quite interesting."

Notice he is present at the show of his thoughts and feelings. He is not responsible for them and he is not they. He is "watching." He is a verb.

UU (THE BOTTOM LINE)

Many outcomes are possible from the process of sitting meditation. A primary outcome is simply to be able to sit and observe from a quiet center all that happens. We discover our thoughts and feelings are not we. This can carry into ordinary life. Our actions are determined not by the cacophony of the periphery but from the silence of the center. We return to being little children. We become quiet centers looking without anxiety but with interest at our miraculous selves.

Every time we walk down the street we are preceded by hosts
of angels singing, "Make way, make way, make way, for the
image of God" (Rabbinical saying).

Practical Matters

How is your time and space working out? Some people I
know have done things as basic as sitting in their car during
lunch hour. Have you been clear you are not to be disturbed? Is
this happening at a moment when the mind is not too full? Is the
space appropriate? Do not suffer. Change what needs to be changed.
This world is filled with noise. Finding quiet is difficult. If the
phone is not off the hook, or the pager is on, you will spend the
time waiting for the ring, even if it does not ring.

Questions and Answers

1) Q: Is what you describe much like the operation of grace?
   Most of us Christians, as you say, seem to be raised to
   judge ourselves. Sometimes I think that we have forgotten to observe ourselves (an others) within the realm of
   the mercy available to us through Christ.

   A: It will feel more and more like the operation of grace as we
   proceed. However, "grace" is a term of later Christians, not
   a term used by Jesus. The doctrine of sin seems distant
   from his picture of the universe. The parable of the prodigal son emphasizes the impossibility of separating myself
   from the father no matter what sinful act I choose. Although Jesus discourages the sinful act, he does not see it
   creating separation. This takes the destructive power out
   of the notion of "sin" and removes the necessity of "grace"
   as a cure for sin. But let's turn back to your questions and

statement. This does not remove the usefulness of the term "grace" to denote the free flowing of the Divine Presence's love through our system. I agree with you that this is very much like grace. Probably is grace.

2) Q: I have allotted thirty minutes a day for meditation. On some occasions I feel like sitting longer. Is it o.k, to let the period run over?

A: Avoid letting the period run over. If you know you are going to sit for thirty minutes, then over time you stop arguing with yourself about when to get up. Once you allow yourself to sit more than thirty minutes, then the length of time for sitting is back up for grabs. Tomorrow or the next day you will be uncomfortable and suggesting to yourself that maybe you should get up sooner. Then you will be considering how many times have you run over in the last week, adding up those minutes and considering subtracting them from this uncomfortable session. Or maybe you could quit early today and add on tomorrow? The mind is enough of a mess. Don't mess it up further.

If you find that consistently you might enjoy sitting longer, schedule yourself longer and stick to it. However, even suggesting that makes me nervous. I usually schedule myself for more of a good thing, just before I quit. This has happened often enough that I think I am dealing with cause and effect here.

3) Q: While I agree that detachment/acceptance from feelings is useful and enlightening, it seems that we also lose some richness—if we are all detached, how do we show enthusiasm, delight, etc.? Wouldn't we be somewhat robotic?

A: I am not talking about shutting down the feeling. If anything I am seeking to become even more aware of it as I am aware of all things. I want to love my feelings. However, through the practice I seek a distance between that which feels, sees, thinks, perceives, conceptualizes, and

judges (to name a few of the functions) and that which observes this happening. I identify with the observing. This
puts me in a quieter place and in a place where I can decide
what I want to do with these feelings. So I feel anger
deeply, but from a distance watching myself feel anger.
And I can decide what I will do with this anger, maybe
watch it trail to nothing. Or maybe shout at someone.

My own experience is that over time I have become
more robust, my temper fiercer and my joy more exuberant.

In such a way of being I become even less of a robot
than in more ordinary ways of being in which my strings
are pulled by that which made me angry and by the anger.
This is the way of the robot. To have my strings pulled.
Or to sit silently stifled by decorum from even knowing
that this moment is excruciatingly funny.

Meditation practice leads to robotic behavior in those
who take it on as a new set of rules by which their strings
are to be manipulated. They take pride in following the
rules and being able to sit long periods watching their
breath. They are pleased to present a perfect "monk like"
set of behaviors to the world. (I put "monk" in quotes because after twelve years of monastic life I know what
monks are really like.) They try to subordinate the reptilian and mammalian minds to the human mind. We are
trying to let the human mind be aware of the others, and
then what will happen will happen.

What does tend to happen is that one becomes quieter,
less noisy, but more intense. But whatever happens happens. We cannot control it.

4) Q: You describe a friend who had a moment of "loving attention" in a supermarket parking lot. Could you describe
this more? Is it like a blind person who suddenly can see?
The optical stimulation is so overwhelming that they
cannot mentally deal with it.

A: It was not a friend but a teacher. After years of practice things like this still happen. The experience is similar to that of a blind person who always lived in a world of blind people and never knew that sight was possible for anyone, suddenly seeing. This was a surprise to my teacher despite the fact that she was teaching people it was possible.

Loving attention turns the world upside down. Or to be more exact, turns the world right side up. It shows us the plain physical material world, which has always been there but lost to our adult eyes. Seeing in this manner awakens us to the fact that we are a condensation of the Divine, flowing into an ambiguous future, not an actor in a play, long ago written. The reign of God is in its depths quite unexpected even when we have been looking for it.

5) Q: When seeing the world in peace and brightness is there any point to continuing meditation practice?

A: Maybe not right then. No harm just enjoying a great way of being that has been given to you. However, like anything this will pass, so continuing the practice will be helpful in allowing it to happen again, perhaps even more frequently. Besides, it is one gift among many that are out there to be given, so don't cling to it. There is more to be had. A deeper and different understanding is possible.

Keep the practice rolling to maintain the habit of practice if nothing else.

6) Q: In class you said that the attempt to not look at one thing dims the perception of everything else. Is it not possible to see something extraordinarily well by fixating on it and ignoring other things?

A: The brightest awareness and the most natural is the awareness of the child, which moves from one thing to another as the child's interest in various things and love for them moves and as he or she continues or ceases to be interested in himself or herself. It is possible to remain interested for hours. I would not call that "fixation" or "ignoring." I would call it ongoing "interest." For most of us, movements, color, shape, attract our attention, but after they have been explored our attention, moves on. In meditation we allow the thought and feeling to arise and then label it and move on when we have had enough. In the best instance, our attention moved on without any judgment on our part. To continue to look after interest has moved on is to look with strained and dull awareness.

When one of our members reports that at her conference she felt bright awareness interacting with the attendees, valued and trusted friends, what I think is happening is that in an atmosphere of safety we no longer put energy into blocking feelings and perceptions but allow them to freely enter our awareness. In a normal conference she would have been disregarding some people because she did not like them, disregarding others because their knowledge threatened her ego, shutting off others because they were mean and attacking, and trying to ignore the fountain in the center of the courtyard that sounds like Niagara Falls.

In an atmosphere of safety, beauty and love all these defenses and rigidities can be lowered. This leads to bright shifting awareness. We feel a deep unity with other beings. We are transparent to one another. This can happen by accident among good friends. It can also happen as a result of meditation in that we will always feel safe because without attachment we have nothing to lose. We love all things. St. Francis even loved "Brother Death." Feel like that and all situations will be filled with bright awareness, transparency, and unity.

And then we will be like a little child, and the adult world will have difficulty understanding us.

7) Q: Sometimes I am depressed for long periods. Is that listed as a feeling? I would suppose so.

A: Things such as depression, cynicism, longstanding anger, blissfulness, are called "mental states" and deserve more room than I will give them here. They are troublesome in that they are not a response to a reality but become a response-producing reality of their own. If you spot your states, you are most fortunate. Identify them, gaze on them, label them, and pray to God they go away. There is a marvelous world out there. Even the thorns are marvelous. Better to respond to it than to be locked in your own head trapped in delusions. Even the delusion called "bliss." Consider seeking the assistance of a mental health professional. You might ask yourself what it is that you are depressing.

8)   Q: I daydream a lot and have trouble escaping it.

A: Don't try to escape it. Make a decision. Look at the daydream calmly and decide *to* daydream. Yes! Decide *to* daydream. Then go forward. Your daydream will disappear because you have become conscious of it and made a conscious decision. So consciousness takes over. And if it does not, enjoy your daydream. Watch it. Try not to become completely embroiled in it. If this does not work, I am wrong.

9)   Q: But if everything is delusion, why have feelings about it and why have thoughts? Just sit would seem the answer.

A: Did I say everything is delusion? Some things are, some are not. Step on my toe and a certain level of pain is as real as it gets. The dishonor and disrespect I feel you have put upon me by stepping on my toe, that is delusion. The fact that the hat you wear is a glorious shade of green is reality. The rule you are breaking by wearing it in church is a delusion. My need for my daily bread is reality. My need for ice cream and cake is delusion.

10)   Q: I have been thinking about the sitting position in meditation and checked my yoga sources. They assure me that the lotus-type position is the best because: The spine is

stretched up, the chest expanded, and the head is held in place. This way the diaphragm works efficiently in a relaxed manner. The weight of the whole body is centered on the base of the spine and distributed though the buttocks. This creates pressure, which creates heat. As the heat increases, the pranic force at the base of the spine expands and rises. Because everything is in alignment the pranic energy flows freely upward. By keeping the head, neck, and trunk straight and sitting in a meditative pose, one attains firmness in the energy that is controlled by the Kurma nadi(the cosmic snake). Sitting in the same pose every day is a way of training our bodies and minds to be aware of the Truth on which we meditate. A correct posture allows us to use the body as an efficient tool for working with the mind.

A: Well and good. But I seek not *samandi* but the absence of delusion. Not the same thing. And I think posture has little to do with it. I can attempt to be aware of reality while flat on my back and do frequently as I am waking up in the morning. Posture has something to do with it, in that sitting so that I stay alert is helpful, but I am not trying to do what the Hindu experts in yoga do.

When a man stands in prayer and desires to join
himself to eternity.
and the alien thoughts come and descend on him—
these are holy sparks that have sunken and wish
to be raised
and redeemed by him;
and the sparks belong to him,
they are kindred to the roots of his soul;
it is his own powers he must redeem.

The Baal Shem Tov

First Interlude

What Am I Doing Here?

From time to time I will insert into the flow of chapters an "interlude." I use these to address issues that arise that do not easily fit into the flow but need to be faced.

The first of these is: "What is the purpose of all this activity?" I don't raise this issue, but some of my students do. About this point many who are dutifully watching their breath begin to wonder why they are doing it. So comes the question "What am I doing here?"

I could respond that I have already told you that. But in the light of the number of people who have missed my rationale, if I have told you, I have not done it well.

I could respond that it is you who decided to begin this, so why don't you recall your motives? They may still be operating. If you can recall your motives, or search for them in your deepest being, those are probably the accurate list of reasons you are still here and plugging away at meditation.

But to stop with that answer appears unfeeling, not caring about your struggle. I will give you the three reasons I think you might want to continue sitting and studying. They are my reasons for what I am doing and they may work for you.

First, I want to learn how to do Buddhist meditation in a Christian setting. In the course of twelve chapters and with three months of practice about the only result I can guarantee is that you will have some grasp of how to do this. Other results come more slowly for most people. For most this has gradual benefits. But this book covers the bases fairly well. You will know how.

Second, I want to live in the kingdom of God. I want to live in a quiet center, conscious of the divine and the infinite in all that rushes around me. I want to walk in beauty. I want to live in the light. I want purity of thought, a compassionate heart, and kindly action to flow undisturbed from the Spirit of God working through me.

Third, since few are allowed the experience of total unity with the Divine that I hope for in my second objective, for my third objective I seek at least day by day to become quieter, to become more conscious of the divine and the infinite in all that rushes around me. To see more beauty and live with more light. I hope to become kinder, purer, and more compassionate in heart and action and to be more open to the nudges of the Spirit.

The first objective will be fulfilled by just plugging on. You will know how to do this by the end of the course. The third objective will be gradually approached over the years. I grow quieter as will you. The second objective may be granted to you or me, or not. For some it happens.

All of the above is a concession to our western need to accomplish. A Buddhist master would have responded to the question of purpose by asking you to just go back and sit. Follow the rules, and then you will see what will happen, if anything. But rightly or wrongly we westerners do not have this type of faith in a teacher. I am not someone who has been appointed to teach the *dharma* by a teacher formed in the fires of eastern monastic tradition. Rightly or wrongly I do not have such a person's certitude about what will work for you. So I have extended to you some possibilities.

I must lay in front of you this one protest. This quiet cannot be achieved. It is achievement and the need to achieve that destroys the quiet. We must look with loving awareness at what is. The kingdom of God is already here. We just have not been looking.

So as concession to your need and my need to know what this reading and practice could achieve, I give you reasons to proceed. But finally, I warn you that focusing on achieving is not the path. There is nothing to achieve. It is all here already. The kingdom of God is spread out before you, and you do not see it. Just look. That's all we are doing. Just looking.

In the first chapters I introduce the practice of sitting, which is looking with loving awareness. As we proceed I place before you descriptions of various delusions that may be interfering with your ability to look, that you may become aware of them and that they may dissolve. My hope is that along the line we may wake up to the fact that we are living in the kingdom of God. Right now. Already. Nothing to achieve. So in a sense we have no purpose.

No "why."
Just seeing what
"Is."

If the doors of perception were cleansed every thing would appear to man
as it is,
infinite.

For man has closed himself up, till he sees all things thro' narrow chinks
of his cavern.

William Blake

5

The Delusion
that Happiness Results from
Fulfilling Desires

Take Jesus Seriously

That's why I tell you: Don't fret about life—what you're going to eat—or about your body—what you're going to wear. Remember there is more to living than food and clothing. Think about the crows: they don't plant or harvest, they don't have storerooms or barns. Yet God feeds them. You're worth a lot more than the birds! Can any of you add an hour to life by fretting about it? So if you can't do a little thing like that, why worry about the rest? Think about how the wild lilies grow: they don't slave and they never spin. Yet let me tell you, even Solomon at the height of his glory was never decked out like one of them. If God dresses up the grass in the field, which is here today and tomorrow is tossed into an oven, it is surely more likely God cares for you, you who take nothing for granted (2).

Explanation

The Buddha was sheltered in his childhood from seeing suffering. As a young man the fact of suffering came to him as a shock, and he cast aside his wealth and position and began to seek its cure. He tried everything including extreme ascetical practices. Finally, in a fit of stubbornness, he decided he would sit under a tree until he had the correct perspective on life. It was under that tree that true understanding came to him. He saw the world as it was. He entered, in our language, the kingdom of God. In his language, he was enlightened.

In one set of stories after enlightenment, his heart went out to humankind, and he felt the need to teach what he had learned. (In another set of stories he had to be talked into spreading the word, thinking that human beings were too dumb to get it.) His beginning formulation of the dharma, his gospel, is the Four Noble Truths.

The Fact of Suffering

The Cause of Suffering: Desire

The Cure for Suffering: Cessation of Desire

The Eightfold Path to Cessation: One of the paths is meditation practice. The others fit very nicely within the pantheon of Christian virtues and practices.

The first Noble Truth is often translated: "That Life is suffering." This is not accurate. He knew as well as anyone that much of life is pleasant. Some of life is pain. We shall return to this in the next chapter.

He distinguished between the inevitable pains of life and our feelings about them. "Pain" and "suffering" are not synonyms as he used the words and as we use them here. Suffering is our reaction to pain. What he taught was that while the pain is unavoidable, the suffering around it is caused by desiring things to be different. If we can become perfectly detached from the desire, suffering can be reduced to absolutely nothing. Pain of course will remain.

The ability to be detached from the desire to escape wracking pain is beyond most of us. Although before we leave the observation of the extreme, let us admit that some who take the Buddha's words very seriously have proven that pain can be put in its place by those who desire nothing different. Real yogis do lie on real beds of nails. Jesus really did accept the cross, setting aside a very normal desire to avoid pain.

Some of us at some time will be called to enter these depths. From root canals to cancer we can expect we shall receive our invitation. Our observations, however, will be about life as ordinarily lived and then about meditation practice.

First, I do not want my greed to drive my life. The American desire for the good life, meaning to have self stuffed with all that can be offered and then want more, leaves us suffering in the midst of plenty. There is no such thing as enough. Possession is an addictive substance. Like nicotine, the more we have, the more we want. Greed leads to no happy country. If that were the whole problem, leading a simple life would solve everything. The simple life is very helpful but desire is subtler than the most obvious greed.

As I ride my spartan and simple motorcycle up a country road outside of my home city, I experience not joy but regret because I would rather be riding it in Northern Minnesota. Last month I was riding it in Northern Minnesota, but I was experiencing regret that I was on the road to Bemidji and not the road to Grand Marais although the month before that I was on the road to Grand Marais, experiencing regret that the trip to the West Coast had to be canceled. At none of these times did I experience the full glory of what I was doing because I desired more than what I had. I was unwilling to settle for loving what was there. So I suffer.

"More than what I had" was unavailable. The "more" that I thought I needed was perfect satiation of my desire, and that is not available. No matter where I ride the motorcycle I will not be perfectly satiated. Nobody is. To think that desire can be satiated is a delusion. The desire for this or that can be satiated. But desire itself then moves on to desire more than what it desired before. Never ending.

I sit on a chair in quiet meditation, the world turned to glory around me. I stand to get a cup of tea and all turns to ashes. I have made the world imperfect for as I sat I had all that I wanted, but I now want tea and I do not have it. I do not want to be a man crossing the room for tea, which would return me to glory. I want to be a man who has tea, and that cannot be without crossing the room. Oh, sadness. I suffer.

In all these instances detachment from my desire would make the problem less. Indeed perfect detachment would make it no problem at all. Instead of rejecting what is in favor of some standard that is not actualized, I would love the situation I was in.

Even there, I can make myself suffer in the midst of glory. My sailboat surges across the dying evening winds of Lake Superior, sunset glowing over the stern, and a piano concerto playing on the stereo below. I do not want it to end. I cling to it. And I suffer.

Desire turns my ordinary life of happiness into continuous suffering. I flee pain, and I suffer. I grasp for more, and I suffer. I cling to what I am and have in the present, and I suffer.

The Buddha achieved enlightenment by sitting under the tree until he did not desire to be elsewhere, until he did not desire even to be there. He sat there until he did not desire.

The delusion that desire satisfied brings happiness makes jackasses of us all.

Jesus said: "That's why I tell you: Don't fret about life—what you're going to eat—or about your body—what you're going to wear. Remember there is more to living than food and clothing. Think about the crows: they don't plant or harvest, they don't have storerooms or barns. Yet God feeds them. You're worth a lot more than the birds! Can any of you add an hour to life by fretting about it? So if you can't do a little thing like that, why worry about the rest? Think about how the wild lilies grow: they don't slave and they never spin. Yet let me tell you, even Solomon at the height of his glory was never decked out like one of them. If God dresses up the grass in the field, which is here today and tomorrow is tossed into an oven, it is surely more likely God cares for you, you who take nothing for granted" (2).

What are we being told here? It is one thing for Jesus to say this stuff to Jewish peasants of his time, but how am I to survive in this society with this advice? This is precisely why we don't take Jesus seriously. He says things like this.

About ten years ago I ran a small consulting business. I lived from month to month on the needs of business and government people to have someone straighten out sick teams. I was loved in the moment of my work, and paid well, but no one really wanted to see me again. I was the signal that things were bad, like going to see the oncologist. One hopes not to.

Therefore my business never was steady. Nobody signed me up to work with his or her group for years at a time. This team now. Fix it. Hope never to see you again. And then six months later, whoops, another one sick, welcome back and we will be happy when you are gone.

What, me worry?

Of course!

My wife was well employed, but we had a big house, three cars, and two children who thought they were going to college on my nickel. Having studied these texts what would I say to myself if myself were to have asked?

"It is admirable that you have set goals for yourself. Go right ahead. We humans do that. It is great that you want good things for your children. Go right ahead. Marvelous that you are out there hustling the business. Proud of the good work you do. But do not wrap yourself around the axle about whether it comes out all right or not. Let that reptilian brain and that mammalian brain spin away with fitting schemes for Tittipu. But you, live up there in that human balloon, looking at it with peaceful love, even as it is happening."

In this we Christians differ from many Buddhists I know. They hope for the *cessation* of desire. I recommend hoping for *detachment* from desire. In the first instance, the desire is no longer there. In the second, the desire is there, but if it is not fulfilled for any variety of reasons my life shall not be diminished. It is not the key to my happiness. I am certainly not going to worry about desire fulfillment. Jesus does not attack desire directly, but challenges the anxiety we experience about desire fulfillment. He grants that we desire to eat. He suggests leaving to the Father the anxiety about whether or not we shall eat. He tells us to desire only the minimum (our daily bread) and to experience no anxiety about what we desire.

Anxiety may be defined as attachment to desire and what is desired. Desire is both free to create the future but loses its hold on my being when I am detached from it, that is, not anxious about it.

This difference of philosophy is what causes Christians to put their energy into good works as well as into self-enhancing endeavors. The Buddhist has no inherent reason to improve the world. Indeed the desire for improvement is but one desire among many that need to cease in this philosophy. A Christian is encouraged to pursue the desire, but free from anxiety about it. The desire has its source in the Father's will. The outcome is the Father's business. Anxiety is to be avoided.

Give your desire the same loving attention you give all other thoughts and feelings. Give the activity in the external world required to fulfill the desire the same loving attention you give all things outside of yourself. Allow it to occur without worrying or caring about its success. In other words do not be anxious about it.

Some Buddhists would say that the more detached you become from your desire the more you will sink to a deeper level of life where you identify with the whole and your desire becomes a desire for the good of the whole not a desire for the good of the little piece called you. Precisely! Jesus died for the will of the Father, not his own desires at all, unless you remember that he substituted the will of the Father for his own.

Part of our Christian heritage is that we are called by God to improve the earth, make it more livable, and by so doing make conscious thought and holiness available to more people. If we will mix the godly drive to create the City of God on earth with detachment from even that desire we will work without anxiety, advancing the goal without trampling on the opportunity to live in the kingdom right now. Even thinking that success in feeding the poor will bring happiness is a delusion. It is a nicer delusion than some others, more useful in its effects, but still a delusion.

An excellent example of how to do it is the example of the well practicing Benedictine monk who works in order to work, not in order to accomplish. He or she allots portions of the day for prayer, study, work, and leisure and does each of these because that is what God desires. (The bell that calls the monk from one event to another is referred to when feeling romantic as the *Vox Dei* or "Voice of God" since by announcing the next moment of the schedule, it announces God's will for the monk irrespective of other needs. When not feeling romantic, monks often call it other things.) In the process things will be accomplished, but the accomplishment is not what is desired and therefore if it does not come about the monk has done what she or he was supposed to do, even without achievement.

Martin Luther's breakthrough insight falls into this pattern. He was trying to be good and to do good. One day while sitting on the toilet (*The Young Luther,* Erik Ericsson,) the insight came to him that it was not his good works that would get him to heaven, but his faith. He gave up in that moment even the desire to do good, and with that release came the peace that passes all understanding.

At the same time, Ericsson, the psychologist, notes, came sudden relief from his life long problem of constipation. What fun, that the unconscious should be located in this instance in the intestinal tract and the sacramental sign of enlightenment be a great bowel movement. It's all in the body.

"What do sparrows cost? A dime a dozen? Yet not one of them is overlooked by God?" (2).

Sparrows get rained on. So will you. Sparrows sometimes cannot find food. Sometimes you will not have clients. Perhaps your children will have to find a different nickel to go to college on. The big difference between you and the sparrow is the sparrows neither desire nor expect, they simply receive what God sends. God loves you. You love God and what God sends. Let it go at that.

Jesus did not only say this, he lived it. Compare yourself to Jesus who could ask people to look at him and how he lived: "Foxes have dens, and birds of the sky have nests, but this mother's child has nowhere to rest his head" (2).

Jesus told us to ask for the bread we need for the day (2), but I cannot even taste my daily bread because I am worried about next year's buying power. Ask for the bare minimum. Everything else is extra, nice, and worthy of rejoicing. But don't expect it.

Jesus assumes a totally unbreakable bond between this Father and us, and it is in this loving bond that joy appears, not in the fulfillment of desire.

Jesus tells of a son who desires more than he sees as available in his father's house, so he takes his inheritance and heads out for the pleasures of life. This inheritance, by the way, was also his father's social security. A good son would have taken it only in due time and would have used it in part to keep his father in the style to which he had grown accustomed. But not this kid. He blows it on drink and prostitutes, which makes it necessary for him to go to work, and since he is not very employable he ends up taking care of the pigs, which for a Jew would be the very bottom of the barrel, caring for an animal he was forbidden to eat.

His desires not being well met he decides to take a risk and see if his father will take him back where he has a better shot at desire fulfillment. There is nothing about love in his thinking. He is after food and clothing. When his father sees him coming Jesus begins to tell the story from the father's perspective. The scenario shifts, language changes, issues flip over. No longer is it about desire, or need gratification. His father knows only one thing: *His* son has returned. The oldest son has his nose out of joint that his dad is throwing a party, and again the father responds to a torrent of complaint about who has been fulfilling whose needs and whose needs should be fulfilled now with but one sentence really and that is: *Your* brother has returned (9).

It is the bond, the union, and the connection that is important. The rest is comparatively incidental. God is our inevitable companion on the way.

The detachment from our own desires, absence of anxiety, leads to experiencing the Divine Presence, which in turn leads to being driven by God's desires. "You can't be enslaved to both God and a bank account" (17). Give up attachment to the desire to fatten the bank account, and we are free to become sons and daughters of the Divine. We cannot do both.

It is for that reason that we are told: "If someone is determined to sue you for your coat, give that person the shirt off of your back to go with it" (3). No clinging to what I want. Let it go.

I entered a University Campus Ministry building years ago to nearly collide with an acquaintance. I had hoped to catch Jim. I was a little lost and would value his advice. Here he was with coat and hat on, in the doorway. He invited me in, sat and chatted for a couple of hours. Well beyond suppertime, as I got up to go, I asked what had been his destination when I met him. "Just going to buy a car. It can wait."

I tell you, not one of my cars ever could wait. Positions reversed I would have run him over rather than change my direction. On occasion I have tried following this advice. Not my will but God's be done. It has felt very good.

In meditation I watch my desires rise and form. If I could but shift my bottom a little life would be without any pain. If the time would pass more quickly then I would not have to sit here any longer but could go sit in my office. If I only had a cup of tea, I would be happy. I watch these desires form, respect them as perfectly valid desires for this human being, and then watch them march off stage unfulfilled. In this small space and time practicing for the serious stuff.

So in life, I see the ceaseless marching of my desires. My little brain is conniving to create for me a future. I do try to make good things happen. But at the same time I look at what my little brains and I are doing with mild amusement well aware that this is not what counts. What counts is that I remain awake to the Divine within me and around me, personified by the word "Father." I accept my own desires. I am detached from them, and it is in that that I find freedom from anxiety, what Paul describes as the "Peace that passes all understanding."

I have found it useful, sometimes during meditation, and sometimes during normal living, to consciously put the future and with it what I want into the hands of the Father. I have been scheming to make something happen. I have laid my plans. Perhaps I am even in the midst of executing them. I experience no regret or shame at this, for that is what we humans do. But then, I do what Jesus has shown me to do. I take in a deep breath and visualize the situation I am working on. As I breathe out, I turn the situation over to the Father.

Not my preferred outcome, but the actual situation. Now I await God's outcome. God may choose to speak definitively through some other verb. Indeed, it may have been my task to voice the wrong answer as a foil for the right one.

My vestry is voting to pursue a course I consider unwise. I have gathered my arguments, preparing for the meeting. I take in my breath, recalling the situation, their anger, their feelings, my arguments, and I turn it over to the Father. This night I will present my arguments. He is in charge of the outcome.

We have been guaranteed, and I can assure you that it is true, that the moment we are free from the anxiety about desire we will find ourselves in deep connection with the Divine Presence. As we look at reality with loving attention, stripped of the anxiety that it be anything but what it is, the reality of the Divine Presence forces itself upon us, for it is the Divine that is the source of loving attention. If we were never anxious, we would always worship.

Cleansed from my desires my heart is now open to other people. Compassion is the fruit of letting go of desire. What blocks my compassion is that I am so locked in my own desires under the delusion that they lead to happiness that I cannot see others except as they relate to my needs to have my desires fulfilled. Others are pleasant tools if they help me and unpleasant obstacles if they are in the way. Cleansed from my desires I now see them, with all their hurts and troubles. Indeed, I see most of them anxious, trapped in their own desires and suffering from that bondage. Compassion and love become my way of life.

Now you may ask what detachment is since it is in itself so excellent. Here you should know that true detachment is nothing else than for the spirit to stand as immovable against whatever may chance to it of joy and sorrow, honor, shame and disgrace, as a mountain of lead stands before a little breath of wind. This immovable detachment brings a man into the greatest equality with God, because God has it from his immovable detachment that he is God, and it is from his detachment that he has his purity and his simplicity and his unchangeability.

Meister Eckhart, On Detachment

Gandhi, when questioned about his life style, said: "I give up everything, and then I can really enjoy it."

UU (THE BOTTOM LINE)

We are taking Jesus seriously when he said: "Don't fret about life—what you're going to eat—or about your body—what you're going to wear. Remember there is more to living than food and clothing." We limit our wants and needs to "our daily bread" and all worry about what will be given us or taken from us we lay on the Father, he or she who mothers us all. We still live life fully, with desire, hope, work, disappointment, but we learn to look at them from the same quiet space that we rest in during meditation practice. We live without anxiety, attachment to our desire. We do not cling to our past, present, or hoped for future.

Practical Matters

Check your posture. Have you gained a habit of sitting straight? Head right over spine. Does your chair support you in that posture? High enough that the knees are below the pelvis? If you are like the rest of us there is a mess going on inside. Help matters by making sure that all is neat on your outside.

Pay attention from a calm center to the rise of anxiety. If you are aware of it as you have learned to be aware of other thoughts and feelings with loving attention, it too shall pass, and if not label it "anxiety." This habit can become immediately useful in normal life.

Questions and Answers

1) Q: But as Christians is not the whole point of this meditation practice that we hope to encounter the Divine Presence. Is that not a legitimate desire?

   A: There is indeed here a double bind. We desire the Divine Presence but to receive the Divine Presence we must be detached from the desire for the Divine Presence. We must watch it with attention as one of the things our kind of human does without requiring for our happiness that it happen. People have reported to me the Divine Presence's breaking through to them in the moment that they gave up hoping for even that.

   The great Buddhist masters insist that one just go and sit, without wanting anything, even a good result from sitting. Sit and give all your loving attention. The problem is that to desire is a function of the person. While desiring I experience my person. My person is a delusion that fills my psychic space and does not leave room to experience the Divine Presence. More on this in chapter eight.

2) Q: Do enlightened Buddhists manage to find their way beyond all expectations of those around them? I can see where this would bring some degree of peace to close relationships, but would it not also diminish the depth of their feelings for others (or capacity for feelings)?

   A: I think enlightened beings come to the spot where they can choose to exercise behavior as a result of their emotions, or they can decide to let the feeling pass without doing anything about it. As a human being I respect my own need to be human and allow myself that. The story is told of the master whose son died, and the day after he was weeping. One of his disciples said: "Why do you weep? You have taught us that all is one, that individuality is a myth, that what appears to be life is transitory, so your son never really was, and whatever he was, was always destined to die. All passes, why do you weep?"

The master replied: "Because my son died."

But back to your question. Is your love for those around you based on their fulfilling your expectations? Life is going to be hard, Sweet Pea.

3)   Q: How do you balance detachment with doing something? We had a situation where we sued someone to achieve a result. If we were detached from the outcome, would we just accept the original outcome and do nothing?

   A: Not necessarily. You can work toward an outcome, therefore implying that you have a desire that it come about, and at the same time be detached from seeking it. To put it one way, your human brain quietly observes your mammalian and reptilian brain conniving to bring about a result. It's what we do to make a living. While desiring and exerting effort at that level, we are just watching at another level, and success or failure means nothing at the level of our union with the Divine Presence.

Of course, the more we observe the less we are motivated to continue the seeking. And the more we seek the trickier it is to maintain awareness of the Divine Presence. A written dialogue exists between Thomas Merton, Trappist monk, and D. T. Suzuki, the first Zen theoretician to capture the American imagination. In one section they are discussing a story from the desert fathers, early Christian hermits. The story is:

A group of thieves robbed a group of hermits. The hermits hunted down the thieves and turned them over to the police. Unsure of their rectitude they sought the opinion of a saint hermit from the other side of the mountain. He dressed them down thoroughly for doing what they had done.

Suzuki said that the hermits had done what should be done. Thieves belong in jail. Merton responded that while thieves belong in jail, hermits should not put them there. Hermits have claimed the Divine Presence and nothing else. Lay people have an obligation to run the world.

So tell me to what extent you are a hermit, and I will tell you if you should sue or not.

It is a great privilege to be a hermit. Even in monasteries few are given it. Lay people choose a more difficult course with obligations to the right order of the world that hermits do not have. I have radically changed my life since I finished helping my sons through college. This level of focus was not available to me while carrying the duties of a father.

Lay people should sue hermits for evading the burdens.

4) Q: This is a lot like the last question but let me ask it anyway. In earlier chapters I was encouraged to look at everything without concept, just seeing what is there in the present, and now I am being asked to move detached from anxiety about outcome. If I do this, will I be successful in the normal world of work, raising a family, making money, and all that?

A: What I am presenting is Jesus' approach to living in the kingdom. We can look to his life for your answer. He was able to respond vigorously in the moment, without worry about outcome. Sometimes warm, sometimes wrathful. He was not a business success, however. If you follow his approach there will be times when worldly things would have turned out much better if you had been either suspicious based on someone's past behavior, paranoid based on past attacks, or manipulative to guarantee a specific future.

That's why Jesus tells the parable of the merchant who sells all for the pearl of great price. Sell suspicion, paranoia, and manipulativeness for the joy of living in the kingdom. You may be successful in worldly terms as well. Or you may not be successful. It's not the point.

5) Q: For some reason this reminds me of the "sharp shooter error." A fellow looked into a barn and saw that the wall was covered with arrows, which had been shot into the center of targets. When he expressed amazement to the owner that he was that good a shot the owner said that first he shot the arrows, and then he painted the targets.

A: I am not positive why this reminds you of that either. However, I find it fits for a couple of reasons.

First, we are trying to have experience precede explanation. Sit. Focus on your breath. Pay loving attention to what comes up. Then look to see if any of the explanations I offer fit. Shoot the arrow, and then check for an appropriate target to paint.

Second, I have shot a bunch of Buddhist arrows into the wall, and then painted on Christian targets based on the sayings of Jesus. This is the way the book has been written. But I am trying to teach the message of Jesus, and only in service to that do I teach the message of the Buddha. Since Jesus was not at all orderly, for good order I must do this backwards and begin with what the Buddha teaches. Adding to the difficulty is the fact that sometimes the messages do not match precisely, although both have a great deal to add to the other.

I have this mess fairly well sorted out in my heart, enough to go forward with it personally. But I do not have it sorted out well enough to present it clearly and concisely. You are stuck with a mess on some of these topics. My only excuse is that often having a mess is better than having nothing.

6) Q: I continue to be bothered by distractions. Will they become less?

A: There is no such thing in this practice as a distraction. Something is trying to emerge and attract your attention. Give it your attention. When I suggest that you label something such as "planning" or "thinking" or "anger," it is not that it is a distraction.

The problem is you have been planning or thinking or being angry with only partial attention. Give it your full attention. It will go away when it has your full attention and becomes boring, and then I suggest for depth that you return to the breath.

Thoughts go away instantly when you give them full attention. For the most part they are fluff. They have little physical content. Some electrical impulses bouncing in the brain. Feelings last longer because they are a mix of abstraction and physical content. Heartbeat might change. Breath shift. Tension in muscles. Physical sensations stick around longer because in their concreteness they are less available to the influence of consciousness. But even itches go away.

Do not think of them as distractions that must be gotten rid of. These become a problem only when you move from awareness of them, to absorption in them. The experience is as if the sensation, feeling, or thought exists by itself and the "watching" that is you has been pulled into it, buried in it. At that point it is useful to label the sensation, feeling, or thought so that it becomes unattractive and moves on.

7) Q: I continue to be puzzled by what you mean by "loving attention." What does it mean to "love?" I run into the word used many ways. What do you mean?

A: I mean "unconditional positive regard." At its subtlest I mean that as something rises in awareness I neither retreat nor neutrally observe, but slightly move toward. Love generally moves toward perhaps even violently. But the love of loving attention is gentle, barely perceptible that it not interfere with what is loved.

8) Q: How about the desire to be healthy? I desire that the tremors of Parkinson's stop. Is that a problem?

A: I am sorry, but yes it is a problem. I say this with caution and respect because of the weight of the burden you bear. But desiring that it be different adds to the suffering. However, the desire I speak of in all of this is a desire that is not satisfied unless it has what it wants. A human desire for health is not in itself the desire I speak of unless you will not rest unless you become healthy. Peace can be found in being here and now a person who has Parkinson's and would prefer health but accepts both these realities. The preference for health and the fact of illness.

—

Be CAREFUL (full of care) for nothing; but in every thing by prayer and supplication with thanksgiving let your requests be made known unto God. And the PEACE of God which passeth all understanding shall keep your hearts and minds through Christ Jesus.

Philippians 4 (King James)

—

6

Distinguishing the Reality of Pain from the Delusion of Suffering

Studying life
I've been noticing
It hurts.

Take Jesus Seriously

Turning to face his disciples squarely, Jesus said:
"Congratulations, you poor!
God's domain belongs to you.
Congratulations, you hungry!
You will have a feast.
Congratulations you who weep now!
You will laugh" (2).

Explanation

The teacher spent an evening discussing pain.

Words mean what we decide they will mean. For this book consider the word "suffering" to mean the problems we make up, the result of the desire for it to be different. They are the delusions: that the end of the world is occurring because my client has let me go, that an itch is unbearable, that cancer means the end of all joys. For this book I will use the word "pain" to mean that which really does hurt. A loss of income has certain very real effects. An itch is an itch. My cancer may very well kill me and may hurt like hell. We can make two errors in the world of pain and suffering. One, we can mistake suffering for pain and allow the delusion to cause us more trouble than the reality. But the opposite problem is also real. We can ignore the pain.

This teacher, a westerner and a psychologist, had entered a Buddhist monastery in Burma and found his practice faltering after about a year. No real progress. His teacher was short on explanation, simply advising him to return to sitting and pay attention to what was emerging. "You are ignoring something" was the advice. So he sat.

His father had been an alcoholic. This had been no secret in the family as he grew up. Later, the college-educated children, including himself the psychologist, had made sense out of the way their psyches had been attacked and compromised. He had many hours of therapy under his belt. He had attended his alcoholic sister's therapist recommended family meeting as she was turning around her life. At this meeting all of his brothers and sisters had been quite clear about the difficulties they were having because dad drank. My teacher at that moment in time knew that he had the problem of having an alcoholic father solved and locked up. He was going on with life.

Then one day during meditation his wandering mind, breath forgotten, came across this overlooked fact. "It hurt." Jesus, God, (or whatever Buddhists say instead) it hurt. Poor little kid had suffered. No way that should happen to a child. Dad sodden in an armchair unable to take him to his ball game. Dad shouting at Mom. Mom hiding the liquor. Him finding it rehidden by his father in his own toy box. Dad showing up at school drunk to the gills. He had discussed all this many times. He had forgotten one great fact among the facts. He had experienced pain.

He wept in the meditation hall. He wept for days in corners of the monastery. "Unfair," his heart raged. "What a dirty trick." Finally the storms died, and his practice began to move steadily ahead. The pain had gone from not being acknowledged, to being seen and cursed, to simply being seen. A fact. He had been hurt.

That being so, on the third night of our retreat, he felt free to bombard us not only with this story but with descriptions of the pain of ordinary life. It hurts to be born. It hurts to be sick. It hurts to be rejected. It hurts to get divorced. It hurts to lose a game. It hurts to fall off a bicycle. Perhaps I exaggerate but the list must have gone for half an hour. (His fellow teacher and wife later suggested that he add one more pain, the pain in the butt he becomes when discussing pain.)

Was not silent endurance the Buddha's motto? For that matter what did the early Christian mean who put the words on Jesus lips: "Take up your cross and follow me." Is that not the religious equivalent of "Suck it up, stiff upper lip, don't cry—be a man?"

Neither Buddhism nor Christianity recommends that you ignore your cross. You take it up. That implies that you know full well what it is and most certainly that it is there. To desire that things be different increases the suffering. It helps multiply the delusion. But to try to ignore pain has the same effect. It is the same thing. Ignoring means that I desire that it not be there. I no longer experience the pain, but I experience the suffering derived from hiding the pain.

Do not ignore pain. That attempts to put it behind, and it will not go there. Immense energy will be wasted trying to stuff it. Give pain the same loving attention you give all things. Loving attention respects the reality that is there. It does not add to pain by piling on concepts that make pain larger than it is. Loving attention does not subtract from pain by trying to ignore its existence. Loving attention respects the reality that is there.

After that *dharma* talk, I had a rough day. Every pain I could remember was reviewed. Every fear I have ever had: dying, suffocation, helplessness, losing my mind, becoming a paraplegic, losing my money, all ran before me in vivid detail.

A rough day. A lousy evening. A restless night. An extraordinary morning.

I joined the other students at dawn, sitting so quietly, my heart barely moving, all at rest, gentle in joy. I, too, had needed compassion. Finally I had taken a straight look at the pains in my heart. Life hurts. It can be borne. It must be borne. It cannot be ignored.

One of my teachers was sitting in the audience when someone asked the Dalai Lama: "What is the fastest way to reach enlightenment."

The Dalai Lama wept. For ten minutes he simply wept. When finished, he did not say why he had wept. Just went on with things.

My teacher had two guesses. First, the Dalai Lama wept as he realized the pain of ordinary life that this person must be experiencing. Second, he wept as he realized this person was looking the wrong direction for the cure and would probably never find the right one.

Pain is burrowed so deeply into our being that sometimes it is not recognized. It is so ordinary that we do not recognize that it hurts. Here are the comments of a student about her experience of basic pain. They were written two weeks before we even took up the topic and therefore represent her authentic insight before hearing the official doctrine.

"An aside for anyone at the sitting on Saturday, I finally realized the reason for the (almost) tears—it came about two hours after I left the church on Saturday. It was always rather obvious in fact—I just failed to make the connection. When I was meditating on Saturday, I was struck by how the physical attachment to my body so limited me. I wondered how often even my own depression was driven by my connection to my body, reliance on neurotransmitters and the like, rather than this part of me (the more or less "authentic" me) that observes all the other mess of me, when I am meditating. I think it was the realization of the limitations of my body that provoked the tears."

Most of us would wave off the fact that our body limits us as an issue not worthy of note. But it is worth note. That is the basic pain the Buddha sees. This extraordinary spirit that we are is stuck with corns and back aches and hang nails, and is its heavy, heavy self. Even on its best days this lump of clay does not move with the speed and grace that my soul hopes of it.

This is why I cannot pay attention in the moment. I view the moment as too dull, boring, and worthless for my attention. This moment is a burden. And indeed it is. I am sitting at a stop sign. I don't want to be here; I want to be at my destination. I am driving the van. I don't want to drive the van; I want to be driving my motorcycle. I am taking off my coat. I don't want to be taking off my coat. I want to be sitting down in the restaurant. I am reading the menu. I don't want to be reading the menu. I want the food to be on the table.

So I do not pay attention to all those irritating moments forced on me by my entrapment in a body and therefore my entrapment in time and in space. If I can come to accept this ordinary pain then I can live into these moments. The stop sign flashes with glory. The van purrs with power, rain bouncing off its solid roof. My coat's craftsmanship and warmth provokes thanks and admiration. The menu is a small work of art providing a universe of the memories of tastes and the excitement of the unknown.

I do not want to spend the rest of my life groaning about the fact that I have a body, but neither do I want to forget that this is a weight I bear.

This is one reason Jesus has a predilection for the poor and suffering. It is that they know they are poor and suffering. Those who do not mourn are not paying attention. Mourning is a doorway to the dawn of reality.

To not see pain in my life is to edit reality. It is to be seduced by a subtle form of delusion. If I edit reality, I shall also edit out the reign of God. If I close my eyes, I not only ignore the monsters, I also ignore the angels. In order to love my body I must love it in its entirety, both as pleasure producing, and pain producing.

Learning to look pain in the eye, not desiring it to be otherwise puts it in its place and allows me to move forward without fear. Why am I not open to the Spirit? Why am I afraid to abandon myself to the will of the Father? I am afraid that the prompting of the Spirit will bring me down a painful path. I am afraid that God's will will hurt.

Look what happened to my brother Jesus. He was big on doing the Father's will, and if there is one thing we are sure of about his history, it is that he ended on a cross.

If I understand that pain is part of life, if I understand that the only way to avoid pain is to avoid life, then when I hear the voice of the Spirit I respond without fear. When I know the will of God, I accept it. It may hurt, but that is what life does. I shall not make it worse by desiring that it be otherwise.

Jesus' promise to us was: "Whoever tries to hang on to his life, will forfeit it, but whoever forfeits his life will preserve it" (17).

A friend of mine was a member of the Milwaukee Fourteen. For those too young to remember, they destroyed draft records in Milwaukee during the Vietnam War as a form of protest. They knew what that would get them: arrest, trial, and imprisonment. Pain.

He told me of the agony he went through deciding to do it. Then he experienced the joy of casting the dice, following through with the action, and living out the consequences. The joy overcame the pain, once the pain was acknowledged and accepted.

This is a paradox of the reign of God that is spread out before you, a truth you accepted in your baptism. You descended into the water as a sign that you gave up your life as you had determined it to be, and you rose out of the water living God's life as he should will it with whatever pain or joy it might bring.

You put on a white garment, signifying that you had entered God's reign, to a life of peace and deep happiness. By losing your life, you preserved it.

Kids are a drag. Aging hurts. Work bores. Sticks and stones break my bones, but words do hurt me too. My body grows tired. My dreams are thwarted. Old age will be a story of increasing limitation. There is only one salvation, and that is to know it.

Jesus spoke directly to his disciples about their choice to become poor, hungry, and in pain in pursuit of the Kingdom.

Turning to face his disciples squarely, Jesus said:
"Congratulations, you poor!"

God's domain belongs to you.
Congratulations, you hungry!
You will have a feast.
Congratulations you who weep now!
You will laugh."

The first time that I realized how deep the connection was between the Buddha and Jesus was when I was reading the dialogue between a Buddhist teacher and his students. He was interacting with one student who just could not seem to get the concept of detachment.

Finally he said: "I want you to look up the works of Meister Eckhart, a medieval Christian mystic. Look up his sermon on 'Blessed are the poor in spirit.' Understand that, and you will understand the Buddha's position on detachment." I looked up that sermon. I was delighted to find from a member of my own heritage the same truth that the eastern sages have tried to teach. Peace is found by accepting what is there and detaching from the need for it to be different.

As you sit meditation do not turn yourself from the pain your body experiences. Your body will become somewhat sore and tired. Look at it with gentle acceptance. Boredom will crowd your thoughts. Being bored is part of life. Look at it with gentle acceptance. Memories will enter your perceptive field of good times but also of bad. As you do not get locked into rerunning the pleasant, also do not quickly slide away from the unpleasant. Look with loving attention at the pain that has been in your life. As your mind struggles with its future, do not try to avoid the ghouls representing where life may take you. Look at them with loving attention. Indeed yes, the fears may become reality.

As with all thoughts and feelings they will come and they will go. That is the way you want it. Not harbored. Not mused on forever. But not ignored.

Neither Jesus nor the Buddha believed in causing pain to self. The Buddha had tried ascetical practice and gave it up for the middle way. Jesus was excoriated for going to too many parties.

It was John the Baptist who spent his ministry on the edge of the desert. Jesus preferred the living rooms of normal people. Indeed, many times he partied with wealthy people. In your practice, and in life, do not seek pain. It will come. Then it is to be accepted.

Perhaps it is only that it is so central to my experience, but I am convinced that if you feel that you are not going anywhere in your spiritual practice at the root of your problem is your unwillingness to accept and detach yourself from the pain, past, present, and future that is blocking your progress.

Blessed are they that weep, are hungry and poor for the sake of the Kingdom.

Take up your cross and follow me.

UU (THE BOTTOM LINE)

How can we who are the poor, hungry, and sad be happy? If we accept that life must be lived without avoiding or even fearing these so-called negative states a door will open for us in that very moment. We take Jesus seriously when he says: "Whoever tries to hang on to his life, will forfeit it, but whoever forfeits his life will preserve it" (17). Let the Father direct our lives without regard to the bumps and bruises, and life will be splendor.

Practical Matters

Are you allowing thoughts and feelings to simply come and go? Or are you panicking every time they come because you feel led astray from success at focusing on the breath? This practice is not about perfection but about seeing and hearing what is. Like a child, allow thoughts and feelings to be the toys mother hangs over the crib when she chooses and removes when she chooses. No grasping. No rejection. Accept what she gives. Loving attention.

This is not the simple attention given by focusing on some thing or some feeling or some thought. At the same time as you are aware of thing/feeling/thought be aware of that which loves and is aware. We are learning to differentiate the observing/loving from the observed/loved and create a space between thing/feeling/thought and response to it, and even observation of it.

Shaq O'Neill is one the worst free throw shooters among the stars of the game of basketball. His coach was asked why Shaq did not practice more. He responded that Shaq practices his heart out, but since he does not understand how to shoot free throws every time he practices he ingrains in himself even more how to do it wrong.

Be careful here. It is time to understand this correctly or practice becomes simply looking at stuff without awareness of the looking itself. In the long run it is more important that we are aware of that current that is looking. In this stream the Spirit influences and the Presence resides.

I repeat: This is not the simple attention given by focusing on some thing or some feeling or some thought. At the same time as you are lovingly aware of thing/feeling/thought be aware of the loving awareness itself. We are learning to differentiate the observing from the observed and create a space between thing/feeling/thought and response to it, and even observing it.

Questions and Answers

1) Q: I was struck by the other student noting the limitations of the body. I've been talking with one of my friends about a sense that we exist as individuals but also as some sort of other thing that is connected to a larger spiritual realm. It seemed to me that the connection isn't limited to being only through Christ, but that we can choose to have that be the way we do connect (I am the way, etc. Is that one authentic?). Anyway, in this meta-world, things that are limiting for us as individuals may or may not be issues. Does this make any sort of sense?

   A: The quote: "I am the way, the truth and the light" is attributed to Jesus by a later author, who is the creator of the quote. It reflects how that author felt about Jesus. Jesus had become the way the truth and the light for him, or her. I think that many of our Christian phrases about being in Christ speak to how someone with our mind map expresses the experience of being one, and also talks about helping everyone have the experience.

That is: that since we are Christian we identify the experience of being one as the experience of being "in Christ," and when we seek to help all other people have the experience we seek to bring them into the Christ. Yes, indeed, because of that we are not limited. We have lost the small identity in which we are mortal, and now identify with the whole, which is immortal.

Other traditions think of the experience of being one as the reality and the experience of everything else particularly of duality, (being two or more) as the delusion. They would say that in daily life one must participate in the delusion of being two in order to breed and eat, but that is not the deepest reality. (They do not exactly say that all is one; they say that all is not two. Not precisely the same thing. That's why there are dualists and non-dualists.)

Our church is dualistic although many of our mystics have been hauled into church court for being non-dualist. You might note if you study this text carefully that I slip from one to the other. In explaining vision the scientists have a particle theory and a wave theory. In explaining spirituality I sometimes use dualism, with God and others outside of me, and sometimes non-dualism, God and others still are not I, but we are seamlessly joined. To indicate that joining I use the phrase "the Divine Presence" as something I experience inside that I expect exists also outside.

With all this talk about what is not the body, I point out that in enlightenment the body will be a clear fact.

Loving the body as burden also means loving the body as joy. Our unwillingness to look at the body as pain prevents us from deeply experiencing the body. When the old masters said that before enlightenment one chops wood and carries water and after enlightenment one chops wood and carries water they were not trying to say that life just continues on as it was before, but the wood and the water and the chopping and the carrying and the body that does this and the spirit that directs it will be present to awareness in a brilliantly different way. (I quote from D. T. Suzuki at the beginning of the Postlude for more on this.)

My own experience has been that early in life to escape the limitations of the body I learned to live in an ephemeral world, of position, and power, and affection, and relationship. I could go on and on listing what I think of as real that is only human creation. In meditation I sink back into the limits of the body and with that become deeply aware of the physical. Then I become aware of my spirit, that which observes this all happening, and then rarely and dimly, I become aware of the greater spirit who is the whole.

2) Q: You end this set of questions with "This is not what *we* think." So my question is, who is this "we"? And if this "we" are Christians, how would you describe what "we" think about this stuff about bad things happening to good people and good things happening to bad people. Is this going to be about "free will"?

A: Yes, the "we" is Christians. Remember the subtitle of the book? Have you forgotten that I am a priest in the Christian tradition? We do not think that the sins of the past generations in any metaphysical way are vented on the present generation. In some ways, of course, they are through establishing historical situations that play out, or shaping a gene pool, or creating family patterns that then effect the next generation. But they do not advance through the generations in the sense of God punishing. Most Christian writers would say that. All should say it. Jesus said it.

However, what I say next is only what some Christian writers would say: We are in the process of creation. Things do not work perfectly. Our creator moves forward over the centuries. In that magnificent evolutionary process, which seems to my eye to be improving the human race, individuals sometimes suffer very bad things. Some very good individuals suffer sometimes because they are pointing out the creator's way in the face of some people behaving very badly. The creator works through us as the vessel of consciousness on the earth and to improve the situation so fewer bad things happen to good people.

To do this one does good things. However, to insure that good things are good, may I recommend sitting meditation? Bringing the mother of all and her will to consciousness.

Could the creator have chosen a more straightforward path? I doubt it. The immutable and all-powerful God is a Greek creation. The Jewish God had a hard time keeping control of the ship. Christian theology has peddled Aristotle's Greek God. The God of the Jews, our spiritual ancestors, as reported in our mythology even had to flood the earth and start over once because things had gotten so far out of hand. Shepherds often argued him out of his plans. Jacob wrestled with him and earned the name of the tribe (Israelites) from God for having withstood both man and God. With this God at the helm I need not rely on "free will" to excuse bad things happening. It appears that God works by creating a mess and then trying to straighten it out. And expects our help besides.

3) Q: Something I learned while preparing for a marathon was: Meet the pain where it is. Do what you have to do in response to it. It is trying to tell you something.

A: Thank you. That does help. I may have implied that pain is simply to be endured. Often it is a signal that can be responded to in ways that heal the body and remove the pain. Pardon my stupidity. I was focused on teaching that the pain must be observed and forgot that some pain is fixable. I had best add that suffering is desiring that pain, which cannot be fixed, disappear. Sure if it is fixable, fix it. May I point out that simply being aware of the pain in its detail removes the suffering and makes the pain more bearable?

4) Q: You refer to thoughts and feelings as passing through, but they really don't, do they? It seems to me they begin and end in me.

A: Just think about it a moment. All thoughts and feelings are instigated from the outside. Either you were told it, or read it, or were pushed or stroked, or are remembering times like that or are fearing times like that. And much of the time in order to pass them on you push or stroke and tell and write, and the rest of the time they pass on without your deliberately passing them to others, but probably without thinking in unconscious ways you do pass them on, many of them anyway.

The way I imagine it is that I am a flow-through tea bag. Water, already colored by others enters me and flows out colored by me. Some of the stain sticks and moves on only reluctantly. The only thing I can claim as me is the bag and tea itself, much as the only thing in life I can claim as me is the bone, gristle, blood, organs, and neurons. But even that was given to me at birth and is in a constant state of modification depending on what I eat, drink, or otherwise inject.

I could say that a chemical imbalance leading to depression is really part of me, but then if I take Prozac and create a new balance am I no longer me? No, I am as much me as I was before, which is whatever a flow-through tea bag can claim as itself.

. In time the bag is dropped into the garbage and even that disintegrates and returns to the flow as the priest used to say to me once a year: "Memento homo, quia pulvis et pulverem reverteris." "Pulvis" is the root word for "pulverize." This puts a little different twist on this warning. "Remember, little boy, that you are dust and to dust you shall return."

This of course used to scare the pants off me. But the more I settle into this way of understanding the more I find life clear, bright, and wonder full.

5) Q: It doesn't seem enough to be aware I'm in hell. (I'm not sure I needed help knowing that.) Where is the happiness? How does the meditation help? I've found it can help with overwhelming feelings of despair and grief by naming them and getting a little perspective, but I was really hoping it would help me be aware of God, Love, and other Good Things. By definition they are always here. Is there any way to increase my awareness of them, or am I stuck just being aware of misery when I'm miserable? Do I get any choices here or is it just observation?

   A: I am sorry. It is just observation. Suffering is in hoping that it be different. You despair because you have a picture of what life should be and you are not getting that. You think God exists only in the joy and not in the misery. If you had no picture of how your world should work and what God is like, then you would just see. And that would be adequate. More than adequate.

7

The Delusion of Permanence

He who
Wears a blue suit
Won't die.

Take Jesus Seriously

To another he said, "Follow me." But he said, "First, let me go and bury my father." Jesus said to him, "Leave it to the dead to bury their own dead; but you, go out and announce God's imperial rule" (3).

Explanation

Groups of humans look at the reality of life they face, work out ways to cope with that reality, and then canonize the ways as the only way real people could do anything. These rules of behavior are what I mean by the word "culture."

A friend of mine got his idea for not only a best selling book but a change in his own life when he was in Africa explaining the wonders of his packsack to his friend, the aborigine guide. Instead of joining him in praise of the sack, the guide shook his head that any man would want to carry so much unnecessary stuff. The guide had a rag to cover his genitals, a staff as support and weapon, a knife to cut things, and a gourd for water. I believe the rag was in deference to our culture and the knife a better way of doing things that our culture had offered him. His father had had only the gourd and the staff. He had doubled his own possessions in one generation, and now his Caucasian client thought all this equipment in the packsack necessary also.

One culture stared at another in disbelief. We cope with the desert by bringing more clothes, more pots, more food, more water, and more coverings. He coped with the desert by bringing less. My friend wrote a book about simplifying, repacking the bag. But that is another, although related, story.

Culture not only teaches us how to deal with the practical; it also protects us from the existential. To be successful in this life according to the world's standards it is helpful to be an existential sucker. Culture protects us from pursuing such existential realities as meaning and purpose. Seeking meaning and purpose is a waste of time in terms of lesser goals. Eventually culture protects us from concern about death.

If we will accept the dictates of culture, we need not think about meaning. As a salesman, I increase sales. Increased sales means increased revenue. Increased revenue makes for increased profits. When I make more sales I get paid more money. When I make more money, I can buy more things for my family and myself. With more things my family and I are happier, and with increased profits the gross national product rises and our nation is better off. With my day-to-day activities governed and protected by these dubious axioms, I need think no further. Just get out there and hustle.

The rat race at all levels has a purpose beyond its most obvious objectives, and that is to keep us from thinking about anything beyond the race itself. Wear a blue suit, and you will never die.

The Buddha listed the sense of permanence as a major delusion. We try to avoid the fact that all things move on. That is why we can ignore our spouse at the breakfast table. We know he or she will be there at supper. The Buddha says that you cannot count on that. No matter how we struggle to make it not so, life moves on.

We are trying to avoid the fact of death. The kingdom of God must be seen through a child's eyes. As a child I was terrified of death.

I remember leaving my bed and seeking my mother to tell her that I was afraid of dying. She reassured me by saying that as you grow up it will go away. You will get busy and forget it. Indeed that is what happened.

I became caught up in conforming. Strove to get through the seminary by being enough in conformance with its culture to be promoted to orders. Strove to behave enough like a parish priest to keep the bishop happy. Strove to look enough like a businessman to have clients. Always performing the cultural activities at least enough to belong and at least enough as to block from my mind the underlying reality of death. My basic striving was to create a delusion of permanence. In the process, of course, I had to forget that I was awareness in a body because that will obviously have to die. So I advanced from the days of childhood by becoming deader and deader in an attempt to avoid death.

Jesus told the story of a rich man who had figured out the best way to invest his fortune for future gain. He went to sleep satisfied and content. Jesus mocked him saying that he did not realize that that very night he would die in his sleep (17). I know that one of the reasons I like to have appointments on the calendar is the underlying feeling of assurance that I won't die because I have an appointment. I can hear Jesus saying, "He had appointments for a year in advance, but that very night he died."

Some see Jesus as an advocate for the poor. I do not know where they read that. He liked the poor. But I do not see him advocating for them. He liked the wealthy also and spent just as much time with them, maybe more.

Some see him as an advocate for the environment. While I think we need advocates for the environment, I have absolutely no idea how anyone could see anything in scripture about this. The passage that springs to mind in which he has something to do with plants is his withering a fig tree because it did not bear fruit on his schedule. Even that story is not on the list of likely historical acts of Jesus.

Read the Gospel carefully and you will see that Jesus did not advocate. He simply lived. He did not work to bring the poor into the middle class. As a matter of fact, he seemed to think they had a better chance of getting the message as poor than if they were making more money. He explained how he lived, but he did not organize to cause others to change laws or even behavior. After you saw him, and heard his explanation, you could walk out the door and ignore him for life.

This infuriated people. Their anger did not come from his forcing them to do it his way. He exhorted, but never forced. Their anger came because he did not do it their way. By doing that he challenged the perfection of the culture. He was messing up the delusion. By doing that he reminded them at a deep level that they were going to die.

He did not obey the religious/hygienic rules about washing his hands before eating. Indeed, he talked back when someone politely reminded him that he had skipped the customary cultural ablutions (14). He allowed his followers to enter the grain fields and gather grain for lunch on the Sabbath (10). For good reason the culture demanded that all rest on the Sabbath, and a good person of the time would have gone hungry rather than enter those fields. This expectation was so stringent that when he healed on the Sabbath he was criticized by the Pharisees, the righteous folk of that time. Surely he could have put it off until the next day (10).

In one truly shocking example, he commends a manager who cheats on the owner of the company because it was the pragmatic alternative to starvation (12).

Several scripture scholars think that the greatest of his crimes was that he was not careful with whom he ate. "He eats with tax collectors and sinners" (8). The culture demanded a hierarchical order. As a traveling preacher he did not belong with this type of folk. Indeed, it appears that he not only broke the boundaries himself but that he invited all types of people to the same table.

If you were a Pharisee who followed Jesus, and some of course did, you too would have to eat with tax collectors and sinners unless you planned to skip supper.

It gets worse. "To another he said, 'Follow me.' But he said, 'First, let me go and bury my father.' Jesus said to him, 'Leave it to the dead to bury their own dead; but you, go out and announce God's imperial rule'" (3).

The dead must be buried. Honor is deserved for their bodies. They will stink. They will create disease. Of course, it is a son's task to bury his father. It is a wise culture that insists that son buries father. And Jesus says: "Leave it to the dead to bury their own dead."

Why are the people doing the burying called "the dead?" They are called "dead" because instead of living they are just following the rules. Doing what one does while awaiting the end of life. Zombies. I do not know, but judging from Jesus' behavior in other circumstances I suspect that if the man had said, "The loss of my father prostrates me with grief," Jesus would have been much kinder. That would be a response to reality, not a response to culture. It would be a response to a breaking heart, not a response to the rules.

Why did people find Jesus upsetting? After all, in the great scheme of things this is small stuff. Telling someone to skip his father's funeral, healing on the wrong day, culling a little grain without raising a sweat, possibly spreading a couple of germs. Why the panic? Why is it frightening to see a person living without delusion in reality?

To understand this we must understand the Pharisee. From childhood on we have heard them put down by Jesus in the Gospels, so we have an image of them as the perennial bad guys. Hypocrites. Whited sepulchers. Jesus was so nasty to them we presume they must have been evil.

They were not.

The Pharisees were a reform movement. They were disgusted at the state of the priesthood. One became a priest because his father was a priest. It was not a process to produce any intellectual or spiritual elite. The priest's work was worship, prayer, and sacrifice. Other people paid a religious tax, the famous tithe, to keep open his place of business and feed him and his family. This was pretty good work. The fact that the quality of the priesthood decayed in place over generations should not be surprising.

The Pharisees were lay people organized to live a more stringent life than the priests' lived or demanded. They wished to return holiness to Israel. They did it by following the rules. They did not even create these rules but found them in Scripture and the law drawn up in accordance with Scripture. These were good people. Family men. Hard workers. Students. Men of prayer.

Here comes this Jesus challenging the very challenge they are making to their fellow Israelites. No wonder they come after him, put pressure on him. In their eyes he was a great teacher giving a lousy example. This must have been deeply offensive to them.

So why does Jesus treat them with such harshness? He himself followed a rule or two also. Could he not understand what they were doing? Why hurl cruel words their way?

Because they were culture bound. They were promoting the delusion. Jesus saw that their way was the way to death. The child's way was the way to life. They were semi-conscious. Not seeing. Not choosing. Run from outside.

As well as being on the wrong path, they seemed irrevocably on the wrong path. He could not get to them. As the Dalai Lama, a nicer man than Jesus, wept at the intractable pain of his questioner, Jesus becomes irritated and harsh in his criticism of those who shield the truth not only from themselves but also from those who might be saved from the pain of this blindness and be ushered into the reign of God. He uses hard words on good men.

What happens when we allow the culture to provide the answers? We can no longer see for ourselves what is happening both outside of us and inside of us. The Buddha insisted that people not take him at his word but look for themselves. Jesus did not want us to take his word that there was a kingdom somewhere that we could get to sometime but to look right now and see it as it is spread out in front of us. Give reality loving attention and bingo! There lies the kingdom.

Parenthetically, I must say that both Jesus and the Buddha would be horrified at the slavish performance of rituals in their names. It reminds me again of the master who said that out of a thousand followers he had only a few disciples. A thousand people followed his rules. A few were looking at reality for themselves. Of the hordes of people who attend church rituals on Sunday, how many expect to be saved by the ritual, and how many are alert to the teaching, seeking the kingdom themselves? To some extent the churches create and preserve the delusions.

When we hear that a person cannot leave a bathroom without washing his hands several times we are concerned. Someone who must avoid stepping on cracks has problems. When our friend must put on his right sock before his left we worry. "Obsessive compulsive" is the clinical word.

What would we feel if there were a group of psychiatrists telling people that life would be all right if they would wash their hands several times, if they would step over cracks, if they would carefully begin with the right sock rather than the left.

Would we feel rage? That is what Jesus felt. Pharisees both secular and sacred exist today with lists of salvific rituals guaranteed by them to bring you to a happy place. In fact they will only deaden the soul.

The kingdom lies out there waiting to be seen. Good people are making it difficult for others to see anything, inducing in them false security and turning them to zombies. We are still doing it, and now we do it in Jesus' name. Fit in. Be a good family person. Be kind. Be polite. Eat your peas. And you will get into heaven.

The culture as an expensive delusion stands between you and the kingdom. It is a defense against the reality of death, but if you rely on this defense it will defend you from the reality of life. Sit with death. When it naturally flows into your mind, allow

it to rest there. Give it even more time than you give to other matters. Consider holding on to it for a moment. It is pain in its ultimate form and should not be ignored.

Beyond this dark door lies the light that has enlightened the
world. No fear. Just look. If there is fear, look at the fear also. You
look as a child looks, ignoring the whispers of the world: "Get
busy, and then you will not notice. Follow the rules and you need
not care." You look as a child looks, with terror that will diminish.
Then you can look as a child who sees in the world not rules and
boundaries but the reign of God spread before her or him.

How to live in this situation, as the Gospel of John says: "In
the world, but not of the world?" I have two hints from modern
psychology.

Everett Schostrom, a psychological researcher of the sixties,
produced an inventory of the behaviors of the deeply happy. He
noted that these people three times out of four respond to their
inner cues for behavior as opposed to outer cues. Put another
way, three out of four times the outside world does not dictate
their behavior.

My first hint on how to live in the world but not be of it is to
pay attention to who is running your ship. How many times are you
doing what others want, and how many times are you doing what
you want? Being inner directed (the term for giving precedence to
the inner cues), will not cause the Spirit to work in your soul, but it
will at least remove cultural barriers to the Spirit working.

The world deluges you with commands from what to buy to
when to smile, from what to wear to when to listen. A friend of
mine once commented that the school system exists to prepare a
person for life. "You mean reading, writing, and arithmetic?" I
asked. "No," he said, "Shut up and do what you are told." To allow
the Spirit to work we must put distance between the culture and
ourselves. At about that same time in the sensitivity training movement people were encouraged to become "participant-observers"
as they walked through life. That is, at the same time as they par-
ticipated in life they held it at a distance and observed what was

going on both in the world around them and in themselves. Watch as you participate. The world's ploys will become evident.

This is a simple extension of meditation practice. You take your watchfulness out of the meditation hall and watch yourself in the marketplace. Watch the thoughts and feeling rise and fall. At the same time watch with loving attention other people tug and pull at your being.

You can be enlightened anywhere, as long as you distance yourself from the siren call of a smothering culture. Accept the culture. Live within it. But detach yourself from it. It is nothing but delusion. We made it up. Some conformity makes life easier, but the deeper work goes on well beneath the level of cultural conformity.

Can you be enlightened without freeing yourself from cultural conformity? I think not. You can look pious by going on frequent retreats and conforming to that culture. But even the culture of those who would be holy prevents the free flow of the spirit. And as long as you are culture-bound in the activities of everyday life it is the culture that will dictate your being, not the spirit of God.

There is no escape from the need to escape.

UU (THE BOTTOM LINE)

The culture is our defense against reality. Distance yourself from the culture. Observe it from a quiet center. Accept the fears it hopes to conceal. Accept the fear of death. Under its veil shines the kingdom of God. Leave the dead to bury the dead.

Practical Matters

How is it going with that helium balloon that is you? Are you able to just float there and let thoughts and feeling, desires and fears, pass you by? Unmoved as a mountain of lead before a whisper of breeze as near to being like God as one can get? Can you from time to time translate that feeling to life in the fast lane?

Not moving, allowing the fast lane to come by? Quiet presence allows us to see the kingdom spread before us.

The insidious grasp of culture is harder to notice while meditating, so you may want to test it in its home waters, the world of everyday practice. Can you decide to do what the culture wants you not to do? Can you decide that without constraint? We have the picture in Luke of Jesus walking through an angry crowd without anyone daring to touch him and with him not feeling obligated to explain himself. Watch him in the Gospels. His decisions neither reflect the prevailing custom nor do they resist it. He invites people of differing stature to the same table despite the norms against doing that but not to spite the norm either. He does it because he wants to eat dinner with them. This can be your sign that you are a free person.

Many a Zen story of enlightenment is the story of the pupil breaking the master's rules. Instead of sitting with the other disciples the pupil approaches the teacher's throne, tosses the teacher onto the ground, and sits on the throne. The teacher gets to his feet, brushes himself off, and bumps the pupil off the seat. They look at each other with glee and march out arm in arm. The rest of the puzzled flock remains sitting, hoping for enlightenment, following the rules.

In an attempt to move toward this freedom, try doing some small thing that, while legal, breaks the operating norms of the culture. Not to show other people how stupid they are but to test your own reactions to stepping outside the limits. Stand on the wrong spot in the elevator. Sit in the pew usually taken by somebody else. Stand closer to someone you are speaking to than people usually do. Sit during the hymn. Don't apologize. Don't smile when you are supposed to. Don't answer a perfectly normal question. Hang up on a telesales' person without explanation. Don't turn right on red. Be silent in a group. Order dessert first and eat it, without explanation. Give a stranger a present.

You may be astonished at the grip over your behavior and feelings your fellow humans have, and in some cases you may discover your unwillingness to let that grip slip. The above examples are of course but minor experiments, not confronting the central cultural rules. You can do that later. This is just practice. This is an opportunity to observe how you feel acting autonomously.

A friend of mine who is a multimillionaire while giving a speech to similarly well heeled souls dropped an offhand remark that he did not intend to collect social security because he had no need for the money. The crowd rose up in indignation that he was not doing what he was supposed to do.

Questions and Answers

1) Q: I've been gestating something, but I am not sure if it has become a question. As irony would have it, for me this week has been full of death. I have been making house calls on an eccentric elderly gentleman who just died last night, and the father of one of our Giving Tree children was shot accidentally in her presence, and a former resident lost a much wanted baby, and a pair of my patients lost an adult son. I'm wondering if loving attention is what gets one through being present to so much grief all at once.

   A: What I am detached from is clinging to emotions that I have or desiring emotions that I do not have. I am living a life of tranquility, and I hear that a friend's father is suddenly dead. I experience a welling of emotion, sadness. It would be clinging to attempt to stifle the sadness in favor of tranquility. I would be clinging to my tranquility. I allow my sadness to come forward at its own speed and stay for its own period of time. Whatever that is. That is detachment.

   At the same time, I watch my sadness with loving attention. Awareness of what is happening purges the emotion of side effects. For instance, I may become aware that I am posturing so that others will see what a good friend I am, responding to the imperative of the culture.

Under loving attention that posturing tends to diminish. Or I may become aware that it is my mother's death that is moving me, and I have lost sight of the immediate source of pain in chasing some old wounds in my head. Under loving attention I tend to come back to the present sadness. Or focus on the older pain and allow that to be healed by attention.

My loving awareness clarifies my emotion, but I make no attempt to manage my emotion. Without lengthening its duration or shortening it, let what happens happen. Things tend to happen differently under the influence of loving attention.

2) Q: If we try to break free of cultural constraints, what are the implications? Isn't almost all of organized religion based on tradition and ritual? When the Last Supper occurred, I assume it was way outside existing rituals, but when we recreate it through communion, is it not ritual and cultural in nature? Isn't baptism ritual? In the extreme, how does organized religion exist in the environment you describe?

A: The "breaking free" is a breaking free from necessarily living in the cultural restraint and viewing the culture's norms as necessary for myself as a human. Religious ritual both comforts and instructs me, and often it allows me to awaken my heart to the Divine Presence. But its richness occurs when I approach it as a free human being, alive and aware of what I am doing in the ritual and not as someone who is simply repeating what my forebears have done in the blind hope that something good will come of it.

3) Q: What do you mean by the phrase "existential sucker?"

A: I find that some people are very shrewd at making day to day decisions but are suckers (easily duped) on matters of existential importance. For instance, they pay little attention to the meaning of life. They will sell their souls for a couple of extra bucks, not realizing that that is what they are doing because it never occurs to them to question the goals their culture sets before them. On the other hand, the fact that they do not "waste" energy on existential matters allows them to pursue the immediate task with ferocity and to experience at that level great success.

4) Q: While meditating I experience a real pressure to be doing something instead. It is as if sitting was a sin or something, and I should be accomplishing, have a product, or help somebody.

A: Congratulations! You have detected one of the devastating lies told by the culture we live in, and you have detected this worm in the center of your being where it does the most harm. You are lucky. You now know it is there.

In Jesus' time the culture said that if you were pure all would be well. In our time, the culture says that if you are productive, all will be well. It makes for a great gross national product but is a lie. Most people are completely unaware that being productive as end all is a cultural construct. They pursue it blindly. Quite a few hear about the lie, think they understand but do not see it working in their being, so continue to be driven by it. Only a few spot it pushing them, and you are one of the few.

Nothing to be done, but watch it. It is one of your ten thousand idiots and will not be banished. But if you keep it under observation, odds are it will govern your behavior less and your life will be more pleasant. Observe it rise during meditation, continue to sit, and observe it passing on. Maybe in daily life you will become more observant of the drive to do things and more relaxed in living, more purposeful in accomplishment.

5) Q: Despite what you said earlier, it seems to me that it makes sense for a Christian to read something, say from Scripture,

and then meditate on it. How can we simply look at what is there with a sense of discovery when we have already been told the nature of reality? Isn't that faith, to know what we believe?

A: We do not know God and therefore don't know with certainty anything related to the knowledge of God. Thomas Aquinas, the great medieval theologian, about as mainstream as you can get, says that it is impossible to know God. Paul the Apostle addressing the Athenians as reported in the Acts of the Apostles tells them that we adore an unknown God one not made from human arts or imagination.

Our brains, which do such an effective job of orienting us in physical space, go wild trying to orient us in metaphysical space. They seek an answer that cannot be given. This is what creates worshipers of idols such as statues, automobiles, volcanoes, stags, family life, professional success, and unnamed millions of substitutes for an unknown God, including dogma. However an unknown God is what we are stuck with.

Therefore, when I sit I can sit with openness to whatever comes up. It cannot contradict my faith because my faith is itself an openness to an unknown God. I do not know who God is or where God is taking me. I submit to the will of the Father. Sitting may make me a little more aware of the nature of reality.

Reading is fine. When I read I learn what others have discerned. It is not the same as sitting and is not a substitute for it.

6) Q: Have you personally had unusual experiences? Do you see yourself as a person of great awareness of reality?

A: When I was about thirty years old, I experienced several hours of what I would call "the peace that passes all understanding," a most unusual and remarkable experience. That evening I was in a meeting with about ten of my classmates. I told them in great detail what the experience felt like. One of them, the class buffoon, said: "But John, that is the way most people feel most of the time."

The other nine said nothing, so I don't know how they felt, but I am fairly sure that what I considered a breakthrough, the class buffoon thought ordinary experience, because it was *his* ordinary experience. Since then it has remained quite clear to me that all I know for sure is that my searching has been rewarded by my having experiences I have not had before and my being more aware of reality than I was before. I have no way to know for sure how my experience relates to yours, or the Buddha's or Jesus' or my mother's.

Often I realize that what has happened is a releasing of a pathological delusion. Am I now ahead of the rest of humanity or have most of them never experienced the pathology and that is why they are unexcited about the possibility of release? I have no idea.

I have had students report to me, with profound gratitude for my assistance, experiences and ways of being I think I have never had. From time to time I have listened skeptically to a famous teacher thinking, "He does not know what he is talking about."

There is a Hindu story of the guru with a great student. The student wondered if he could walk across a river filled with crocodiles. The guru assured him that if he would focus on his breath, center himself in peace and calm, he could jump from crocodile head to crocodile head across the stream. The student did as told, and indeed he crossed safely. Unfortunately when the guru tried to follow he slipped and was eaten by crocodiles.

All I am certain of is that my unusual experiences are unusual to me. You may be ahead of me on the path.

However, I get to write the book. When I was a senior in high school I was made aware that no one could read my writing. This led to a major breakthrough where I became aware of typewriters. So now I am ahead of many a guru because I can type faster.

———

Hear my prayer, O Lord,
And give ear to my cry;
Hold not your peace at my tears.

For I am but a sojourner with you,
a wayfarer, as all my forebears are.

Turn your gaze from me that I may be glad again,
Before I go my way and am no more.

(Ps 39:13-15)

———

8

The Delusion of Person

Take Jesus Seriously

Whoever tries to hang on to life will forfeit it, but whoever forfeits life will preserve it (17).

Explanation

It is always a danger
To aspirants
On the
Path

When they begin
To believe and
Act

As if the ten thousand idiots
Who so long ruled
And lived
Inside

Have all packed their bags
And skipped town
Or
Died.

Hafiz

The way Jesus put it was, "When an unclean spirit leaves a person it wanders through waterless places searching for a resting place. When it doesn't find one, it says, 'I will go back to the home I left. It then returns, and finds it swept and refurbished. Next, it goes out and brings back seven other spirits more vile than itself, who enter and settle in there. So that person ends up worse off than when he or she started" (5).

At this point in our study it is very important that we realize we are not trying to cause the ten thousand idiots to either skip town or die. We are simply trying to see them with loving attention. We accept them, and then we detach from them. If we think we have killed them, we have probably buried them alive where they will stir restlessly deep in our bowels driving us to acts we cannot understand for motives hidden from ourselves.

This is critical now because we shall look at what it means to accept but then detach from our notion of being a person. We are at the very roots of the issue here. We are about to realize that the idiot who has been running the gang of idiots is not us. He is our creation, or in other words, a delusion. But he is a delusion that will struggle to hide from us, remain in existence, and continue to run the show.

Early in life we shape ourselves as persons trying to select a set of characteristics that will work in the culture in which we find ourselves. In my family of origin, silent persistence worked best for me, so I have chosen to be a silent persistent person on things important to me. I know people for whom constant yapping got them what they wanted as children. They now are yappers. One friend of mine learned that being irresistibly cute was a winner. She remains so in her fifties.

We continue this process of creating our person through our schooling. Lawyers learn the skills of a lawyer, and they learn the attitudes. They learn the legitimate arguments in court, and that arguing is the way to live a life. Social workers learn how to pull societal levers to get their clients what they need, and that lever pulling is a marvelous idea. Priests learn how to preach and learn that preaching is always and everywhere the solution to problems. (Since I consort with preachers a fair amount, you hear here a pet peeve.)

The answer to "Who am I?" can be "The who that I have constructed." The process of meditation can bring me one step deeper to the point where the who that I am is the who that is observing with loving attention the who that I have constructed.

To think that we are whom we have constructed is a delusion. We may hold tightly even desperately to that delusion but it is a delusion nevertheless. It is the delusion we reject in baptism when we die to this self and allow Christ to live in us.

It might seem that I am teaching a Buddhist notion contrary to Christian thought because we emphasize so much being a good person, and therefore being a person. But in our baptismal ceremony we say we die to who we have been. If I am able to shed this person, die to it, how ephemeral it must have been. Christianity and Buddhism walk side by side on this issue. You and I are not called to be good; we are called to shed a false sense of identity and wake up to life in God.

One day I took a nap in the middle of the afternoon. Sometimes I wake from these not knowing where I am. This time the sleep must have been even deeper. I woke not knowing who I was. This forgetting took nano seconds only. It is hard to continue to forget your own name. But glorious nano seconds for I was all possibilities in that moment. I could be anyone, do anything. Life was an explosion of glory.

Then I remembered who I was, what my history had been, what my skills are, what kind of human I am, and I climbed back into my box. Disappointed. For a moment I was free, but now I was again trapped in my delusion. I was afraid to abandon it.

Jesus was standing in a crowd and somebody pointed out to him that his relatives were outside. They must have traveled on foot a good distance to come and hear him. What special accommodations did he make for them as a reward for their effort? He said: "My mother and brothers—whoever are they? Whoever does God's will, that is my mother and brother and sister" (11).

At another time he is quoted as saying: "If any of you comes to me and does not hate your own father and mother and wife and children and brothers and sisters—yes, even your own life—you are no disciple of mine" (11).

(There is a similar passage from the Buddha. He urges that you kill all those people.)

What Jesus challenges in me is my need to achieve an identity as a good son, good husband, good father, and good sibling. These precious delusions that I am Ruth and Charlie's son and Jeanne and Mary's brother and Edie's husband and Ben and Dave's father are characteristics of my person and stand between me and my entering the reign of God.

In a sense, these relationships create my sense of person. My relatives (and my friends) claim to be mirrors, showing me who I am. They reflect, however, not reality but the hologram of person that I have constructed, reinforcing the chimera's existence as being a true object. But even "my" hologram was constructed by them as they told me who I was to be. My sense of person arises out of my interaction with those with whom I have serious relationships.

Relationships are constructs. In bare reality, that which is seen by loving attention, I have no "father, brother, wife, mother, sisters." Indeed there are real people outside of my body with whom I have the histories designated by those words. But all that is in the past. If I hope to enter the kingdom, in my present "now" I focus on who is there, and what they might want, not on their relationship to me.

A thirty-year-old male student told the following in class:

"Because of my reading in this class . . . When my mother came to visit last week for Thanksgiving I looked at her without the screen that said she was my mother. I was shocked to realize that 'I don't know this woman.' But I could look at my mother without the screen with loving awareness. I did not know who she was. But I could really watch that woman who was there as she lived in my house."

Jesus has reached to the nub of the issue here. We can surmise from this how he would feel if we told him that we must remain cute, charming, yapping, tender, tough, persistent, or even be good lawyers, doctors, priests, and social workers because that is who we have trained ourselves to be in the past. His example is to take the most basic of the cultural roles that penetrate and form our personality structure and to say that one who clings to them cannot be his disciple and cannot enter into the reign of God.

I suspect that he did not think this out. He was neither psychologist nor philosopher. The scholarship indicates that he had a rocky relationship with his relatives. They thought him crazy and resented him (Prologue). He may have experienced the freedom from having his relationships define his being accidentally. He had to cut them off to be himself. It may have been obvious.

He challenges our sense of person by challenging our sense of the relationships, which form that person. He also challenges our sense of person by challenging our right to the things this person owns.

His statements on "giving" shock us. "Jesus advises:' Give to everyone who begs from you'" (17). "Jesus said: "If you have money don't lend it at interest. Rather, give it to someone from whom you won't get it back" (17). Try this experiment. One day give senselessly. Capriciously. To strangers and friends and enemies. Someone admires your tie, give it to him. Give your teenager ten bucks before she asks. Make breakfast for your spouse. Let someone into line ahead of you. You will experience a joyous breakdown in the wall between you and the universe.

This is beyond the pleasure you will receive because of gratitude. It is the pleasure of breaking out of the cage of personhood, penetrating the walls of the prison. It is perhaps for this reason that the early Christian voice urged us to give in secret that our heavenly Father who sees secrets might be the one to reward us. Without even the return of gratitude on the investment of giving, the walls come tumbling down.

Giving is a sacrament. (When done freely, not like at Christmas or on secretary's day.) A sacrament is an external act that produces internally what it signifies. A free gift indicates that I do not regard something as mine, and there is no me to hold on to things as mine. So if I give, in a sense I give because there is nobody there to give. If I truly act that out, then there is nobody there giving, and suddenly I am living in the kingdom. The reign of God has come upon me. Being denied has defeated the sense of person. The delusion of being a person has washed away in the waters of generosity.

A friend of mine took his wealthy but highly dysfunctional family to a homeless shelter on Christmas Eve. The Ryans grudgingly had committed to put four brothers, their wives and children, sixteen in all, to the task of buying, preparing, serving, and cleaning up for sixty people. Sixteen uncles, aunts, and cousins, instead of experiencing the lust for gifts, the desire insatiable, lived one whole memorable evening in the kingdom. All of their precious delusions about who each of them were and why that was superior to the others broke down in the process of giving. In generosity God gives directly with no person as intermediary.

In the sixties I had the opportunity of frequently serving on the staff, and frequently leading, a human relations workshop called "Creative Risk Taking." The risk participants were encouraged to take was to select a personality characteristic that they considered central to who they were and for the length of the workshop behave exactly the opposite of the way that characteristic should be acted out.

Engineers spent time counseling others. Psychologists withdrew from human interaction, explaining that they were not competent to discuss life with others. Shy people turned off the television in the middle of the Super Bowl, risking the wrath of football aficionados. A nun wore sexy clothes and found out the pleasures and pains of being an object of lust. Macho men asked for help and found out that being comforted was a pleasant experience.

Whatever they chose was immaterial as long as it was something they saw as a piece of their identity, a way in which they and others had defined them in the past. When they pulled that pin, other pins fell, and we all found ourselves functioning without much of a personality structure.

We experienced the raw freedom of the children of God. As the freedom grew good things continued to be done in abundance. From caring for one another to cleaning the common room, one of the free children of God would rise to meet the occasion not from obligation but from the joy of being of service to another. The spirit of the Divine Presence seemed to sweep through the group as insights were shared, acts performed, well beyond what any individual operating on his or her own person could have performed.

And this was not a religious workshop. We never said "God" or "Spirit." We simply encouraged people to forget who they thought they were and allow whatever was left to direct the action.

This is not about being a good person and suppressing my ego. Jesus did not say that losing my ego would be a key to entering the kingdom, but that losing my life would show me the doorway. I am not affirming my person and denying my ego. I am seeing that what I call "me" is a construct and a delusion.

This is not just about my image and the fact that under my image lurks a shadow side of parts of me that are real and I have denied. Indeed, I do have an image, and in creating it I have chosen to deny aspects of myself. But this is no limited field of aspects. It is not that there are several things I could be that I have chosen not to be, but that I could be all human things, and I have chosen only a few of them to be my person.

If I step aside from controlling the boundaries of what I call my person to allow all human possibilities that I might be to float into the presence of my helium balloon, I will discover that I have the potential to become a rapist, or succeed Mother Teresa. It is all there, struggling for awareness and maybe actualization, and I have selected a small field and said: "That's me."

At one point in my life I struggled to keep my behavior consistent. Now I realize that consistency in personality and person is just a struggle. The boundaries of personality and person are fiction and difficult to explain. Now people in one place I frequent know that I hate to hug. In another place they know that I love to hug. For some reason that I have not figured out, I feel differently about hugging in the two places. Why must I become a hugger or a non-hugger? Declare myself once and for all? Ultimately the purpose is to make life easier for both my friends and me. Then we will both know who I am and be protected from surprise and other signs of life.

Teilhard de Chardin, the Jesuit theologian and paleontologist in his books, particularly *The Phenomenon of Man,* writes that there is no other way to understand the ordering of life over the millennia than to realize that consciousness has been trying to emerge over time. From the first piece of protoplasm floating in the scum through fish, apes, and whatever until now, the human being's consciousness has been gradually refined, finding in each succeeding form a more fitting vessel.

When we look at the human race, we see consciousness as fully developed as it ever has been. But we do not identify with consciousness as a whole; we identify with our little piece of it, that which can be encompassed by our own sense of ourselves as a person. The person who becomes nobody lives from the whole, not from that small part called John, or Mary, but from "the Christ" to use the Christian formulation of what this whole should be. "I live now not I, but Christ lives in me," said the apostle Paul.

In this practice we not only detach from our sense of person; we also accept with loving awareness its necessity. We cannot act without in some way becoming a person. In the quiet of meditation some of us can experience ourselves as the whole, or at least as more than we are when person bound. But we cannot act without choosing some pattern of operation.

It would simply be too hard to face every day with every movement a source of free choice. I do many things because that is who I have constructed. I have made a life decision to normally be kind, to normally be on time, to normally fulfill my wife's wishes, to pay my taxes, and to vote.

To accept and to detach from that is to regard what I do normally as not what I do necessarily. Sometimes I can decide to do otherwise. Always I can regard what I am doing with the good-humored detachment of loving attention. Always I can realize that I need not be locked to this part, but that the part is a way I have of dealing with the overwhelming reality that I am part of the whole. Certainly I will cease to harbor contempt for the villains of our society once I realize how close to actualization is my own villainy.

My friends and acquaintances gave me much credit for being a good father, particularly for attending one son's hockey practices and games and the other son's Tai Kwon Do training and tournaments with religious diligence.

Detachment does not mean that I quit going. Detachment means that with a chuckle I realize how important being a "good father" has been to me. I understand how much joy I get from it. Pleasure in performing the duty and pleasure in watching my sons perform in such a way that I can further claim that I am a "good father" because demonstrably they are "good sons." There is nothing wrong with this. I have to do something with my time, better this than an ax murderer.

Nothing wrong with enjoying all aspects of being a person, as long as I remember that that person is simply the chief idiot among the gang of idiots and requires constant loving observation from the quiet eye that is me. From time to time I find it valuable to be a lousy father. It reminds me that the game is a delusion.

Who then is left if we no longer identify ourselves with the person we have tried to construct? Only that helium balloon floating and observing remains.

We are on the same path as when we began, just moving deeper. We thought we saw the world outside us, but from the meditative stance it is possible to accept that most often I see my own concept. Then it becomes possible to detach from it, see the concept as delusion, and on occasion experience more of the richness of what is there.

We identified with our feelings and thoughts and then learned to back up a step and watch them wander across our stage. Particularly we learned to allow desire and pain to enter our awareness without seeking one or fleeing the other. Learning to watch without response. "Loving attention" is the key phrase.

Then we learned to look at our culture, the rituals of life, and realize to what extent it is an artifact of humans building a world that we can live in. To realize, accept, and let it be.

Now we do the same with "who we are." Even that floats outside of our center leaving just me watching that person called John performing in the world we have for the most part created. Me giving loving attention to "me."

What a funny but truly marvelous fellow this person I have constructed. I have carved off a piece of the Divine Presence and called it "John."

> I am God's eye
> Sedately watching "John"
> herd my idiots.

UU (THE BOTTOM LINE)

"Whoever tries to hang on to life will forfeit it, but whoever forfeits life will preserve it" (17). If there is really nobody home, then the Spirit of God can influence the traffic by giving all that is rushing around loving attention.

Practical Matters

Are you still sitting? Or have you given it up in favor of just looking at these words roll by on the page. The words mean little compared to the sitting. Some might sit with much less explanation and do quite well. The words can help but they will help more if you are still sitting.

We are not simply trying to be aware of what is around us or even what is in us. We are trying to be aware of the awareness itself. Experience yourself as that balloon. Feel yourself inside yourself watching yourself.

Beome aware that when you are quiet and empty then these are God's eyes looking out through your body at the universe. You are not a noun. You are a verb. You are: "Watching." "Loving." "Attending." God is the noun.

As I sit I try to be watchful that "John" is trying to become the noun. As feelings and thoughts arise how often they arise to create or protect "John." I feel anger, for "John's" dignity has been insulted. I am planning that "John" may be a success. I would like to scratch my itch because "John" cannot stand it a moment longer. In everything that arises look also for the arising of that noun that would like to take God's rightful place. Do nothing about it for whatever tries to do something then becomes the noun. Observe the noun's rising. Some glorious day it will be too ashamed to emerge as a shadow from shadows.

An Experiment

Pick out a characteristic of yourself that others would say is central to your personality structure. Behave differently a few times.

If you are known as kind, try being mean. If you are generous, try being grasping. If you are neat, try being sloppy. Feel free also if you are sloppy, grasping, and mean to try being neat, generous, or kind. The point is to test the reality of this construct you call your person. Proceed cautiously. There is dynamite here. Run an experiment and see how it feels.

Being stuck on who you are and how you behave is being stuck. This is true even if you are stuck nicely. Our mistake as Christians has been to try to be nice people. That is precisely what the Pharisees were trying to do.

There is a lovely news photograph of several world religious leaders at a conference. For some reason Bishop Tutu, one of my brothers in the Anglican Communion, known for his magnificent struggles in South Africa, is in a wheel chair. The Dalai Lama stands directly behind him and at the formal moment of the official portrait has tipped Tutu's hat over his eyes. Tutu seems to think this is funny. Have these fellows forgotten who they are?

I rather think so!

Questions and Answers

1)   Q: I have difficulty with the paragraph that begins "What
Jesus challenges in me is my need to achieve an identity
as a good son, good father. . . . These stand between me
and my entering the reign of God." I would think that by
being that kind of a person (i.e., good son and father) that
a person would be welcomed into the reign of God. Could
you help me with that one?

Later in your reading (along the same line) you speak
of behaving differently. I have tried to do that, but with
things I think will help me get closer to God. I try to get
rid of the bad behaviors. I don't understand how we can
ever be "stuck nicely." I agree Jesus wants playful people,
but where is the line? Sorry, but I was brought up very
Christian, and some of these fears die hard.

A: Let me first of all confess how difficult I find not being
nice. I was brought up more Christian than you were, if
that is possible. However, that does not really make the
difference because all religions that I know try to educate
us to be nice. Come on a Buddhist retreat with me, and
you will see more niceness than you can bear, or at least
than I can bear.

So what's the problem? Our masters told us something different. That is the first problem. The Buddha
said that if you meet the Buddha on the road, you should
kill him. As quoted above he also favored killing your
closest relatives and Jesus suggested hating them. Jesus
ignored many of the rubrics of niceness in his daily life.
So what is going on here?

Close your eyes and place your two hands together.
If you want to know that they are two hands the simplest
thing to do is rub them on each other. The spot where you
experience the rub is the spot where one is not the other.
We are trying to find that child within us that will ex-

perience the kingdom. We distinguish ourselves from outside reality, from our thoughts and feelings, our sufferings and desires and then are we done? Have we peeled the onion?

Is this lovely person who cares for children, earns money, plays the piano, wears a ponytail, preaches to the faithful, drives without sounding his horn, the essential me? If I will perform an experiment, blowing my horn, cutting my ponytail, telling my children that they will have to find their own way to hockey practice, in the midst of the disapproval I will receive from all quarters, I will experience another layer of my own being. One that simply observes the preacher, driver, ponytail wearer with calmness, care and love and is capable of reversing all those features in the blink of an eye.

This is not a nice man, not an evil one either. But this is the central core on which the Divine Presence will work. This is the target for the Holy Spirit. (So says Meister Eckhart.) During meditation practice I remind myself to go deeper by saying: "Who are you before you say 'yes' or 'no'?" I have an existence prior to being either "nice" or "nasty." That is my true identity and as the Zen master might say "my original face." This is the Holy Spirit's workshop.

2) Q: The great master of the modern stage is Constantin Stanislavsky (1863–1938), actor and mostly director of the Moscow Art Theater. Though Russian and very "Western," he would have resonated deeply to ". . .the who that I am is the who that is observing with loving attention the who that I have constructed." One of his most important and fundamental theses is that, whatever role an actor is playing in whatever play, to be effective he or she must always maintain a kind of third eye (the other two "eyes" being his/her own and the audience's) upon

the action, as if it were the director's "eye." Stanislavsky's "awareness of what is" he called "concentration," e.g., while he was acting at his best, he tells us in his autobiography he was aware even of the mice crawling around in the walls of the Moscow Art Theater.

A: Interesting. As an amateur actor I became quite aware that it was not that John pretended to be Brutus but that the one who was pretending to be John in normal life was about to go on stage and pretend to be Brutus. But if in normal life I did not pretend to be somebody I would just have to sit and be fed intravenously.

3)　Q:　I am confused about your terms and definitions. It seems to me that "ego" would be a better choice than "person" for what you discuss in this chapter. Further, you say that I should "be a verb" and that to see myself as a noun is a delusion, yet a helium balloon is a noun. You address us in class and in writing as if we were nouns. You refer to yourself as a noun. What gives?

A: Sorry about the confusion, but this is not easy. I need a word for that aspect of myself that seeks my own good. I use the word "ego" for that. It seems to be the popular understanding. If you have psychological training this will be confusing because indeed technically what I call "ego" might be the same as "person." Accept my definition for my purposes, please. Then "ego" is a part of being a person. When you sit and when you watch, you will come aware that "ego" is only one of the ten thousand things running around in you. It is not just "ego" that Jesus asks us to lose. Becoming aware that it is all "not me" and that the word "person" used to designate me does not apply is close to the last insight.

However, in describing this most of the time I speak of an infinitesimal "you" doing the watching. This is for ease of conversation. There is no "you" but just "watching. Experiencing this will cause "you" to dissolve into the one. "You" will see "God." The source of all is the Divine. The Divine is the noun. I am the verb.

Some yogis never say "I" in speaking. They will refer to "eating happening." Not that they are eating. This feels awkward and silly to me, if existentially correct. When I am in constant contact with the Divine, I will consider speaking that way, although Jesus did not. Except for rare instances I am deluded and think that "I" exists. So my conversation reflects that delusion. Just think how much you would hate me if I solved this the other way around.

4) Q: What is the relationship of this teaching to being a transparent self?

A: The Buddhists I know and read are not interpersonally oriented. They do not talk about how one person relates to another. However, as I think you must realize otherwise you would not ask, that if you are not inclined to let others know what is happening within your body, you are less likely to be aware of it yourself. I suspect that a couple of TV evangelists would have been less surprised at their sexual urges if they had been in a place where they could have told someone else that they had them. An intention toward personal transparency under reasonable circumstances is a great aid to loving awareness of all that is.

5) Q: It seems that what you are teaching is so idiosyncratic that it cannot be passed on. The unifying web is that this is stuff you know from what you have experienced and read. The above answer touches at least on three fields of knowledge, and you are one of the few to have touched all three. How do your teachings continue?

A: They don't.

What you are colliding with here is one searcher and his accumulated knowledge. From that you take what you take, add it to what you know, and bounce forward, colliding with other billiard balls, influencing and being influenced.

This actually is the Buddha's way. He did not intend the slavish imitation or attempts at imitation that occur in his name. The story is told that he got up from his deathbed to pass on one last lesson. "Don't take anyone's word for it, even mine."

He wants you to be your own experiment. What the Zen masters say to one searching for a teacher who will give them all the answers is that you are seeking a head to put on top of your head. You already have a head. Use that one.

Unfortunately, since the Buddha was a great man, he created generations of people memorizing his system. Jesus never wrote nor did he teach systematically because he too belonged to the billiard ball school of instruction. But he too was a great person, and as such generations have tried to slavishly imitate him. Since I am a small man, you know immediately that you are still on your own. I am happy to help. I shall struggle to stay small. Such an effort.

6) Q: This is the second time you have reported a great insight while waking from a nap. Should I give up meditation and focus on taking naps?

A: The great Hindu teacher Jean Klein suggests almost precisely that. He debunks meditation practice in favor of being alert to the surprise of existence in such moments as waking up, or moving from one moment of focus to another. In such moments there frequently appears a quiet emptiness that can alert you to the fact of being. I would suggest that you continue meditating but be alert to what happens in such times. Once you have spotted reality you experience its sweetness more often.

And you thought you were joking.

7) Q: This gets to be too abstract for me.

A: This may not be your bucket of tea. I am comfortable playing around in this world and completely lost in the physical world. Any room I live in stays precisely the same except for the decay of the years unless my wife insists on redoing it. Then I am totally surprised that a coat of paint can change everything. I just do not see either dirt or possibility. So I understand if this does not suit your way of looking at life.

All of us are competent in some areas and weak in others. Much can be gained from the practice of meditation without all this description. Many of the masters avoid all of what I am describing. They focus on how to sit. Period. You may want to put this on the shelf and read Shunryu Suzuki. He avoids this level of conversation in favor of things like where to watch the breath and how to hold the spine.

I would insist however that this is not abstract. It is subtle. There is something going on in consciousness that can be noticed and described. Feelings can be experienced rising and falling. From where do they rise? You and I can watch and see if we can see. If we think we see we can describe. We are not making this up. We can be wrong about what is going on, or differ in our opinion about what is going on. But something is going on, and it is not an abstraction.

When a physicist insists that what we experience as solid matter is really energy she is not speaking of an abstraction, she is speaking of a subtlety. In precisely the same way I am saying that what you and I think of as "person," solid being, a noun, is really "energy," porous being, a verb organizing other verbs.

At one point in this journey, (the journey of life), self (a sense of person) comes forth, contributes what it can give, then fades forever beyond reach. Self then, is part of this movement, a part through which all men must pass, and the only aspect of the movement for which man alone is responsible. But just as everything must change, the self too eventually disintegrates and dissolves into nothingness. The only thing we know that never changes or passes away is the movement itself.

The Experience of No-self, Bernadette Roberts

Second Interlude

The Delusion of Two

The following is my answer to the question of dualism or non-dualism. Am I a person independent from others or am I not? The essay was written years ago and not in response to the question but in response to reality as I experienced it. I am not sure if this counts as non-dualism to a Buddhist, but whatever it is, it's as close as I get. Note how in all of these normal instances of life, and in the one fictional account, that which is spoken cannot be attributed to the one who seems to be speaking. Either the community is speaking, another person is speaking, the family is speaking, or the Spirit is speaking.

So how can we be two if we speak with one voice? Or how can we be a person when another person controls our vocal chords? Is it not simply energy flowing through what appears to be solid? When billiard balls collide, the energy passes from one to another which then moves forward driven by the new energy and whatever energy it had previously. Who is the "who" who owns the energy? So you influence me, and I move forward influenced also by the sunny day, what my Latin professor taught me, and mother's admonitions. So am I a separate "I"? And what is the name of this energy if not "the Spirit of God."

Indeed, some scientists attribute our sensation of consciousness, spirit, and being one in the spirit to the fact that our muscular structure, particularly our facial muscles, make it possible for us to communicate subtly to one another. So what we take to be our individual consciousness rises from our existence within a group.

(When I wrote this, the point I was trying to make lies in paragraph one. The others are parallel. "Fives" are similar, as are "fours" and so on. This mimics a literary style supposed to have been used in St. John's Gospel. Don't let it bother you.)

The Choir

5) At St. John's Abbey, the cantor, while reading the psalm, does so with no inflection, as speak the monks in responding. That is because it is important that the monastery prays but it is unimportant that the monks pray. It is an insult to tell a monk that his voice was heard in choir for the fervor of his individual prayer may have broken the peace of the whole. So the cantor, sixty and balding, with a heavy German accent, leads all the monks, most in black robes, by intoning, "O Lord, open my lips," in a tone of ultimate boredom. And with similar boredom seventy monks and I respond, "And my mouth will announce your praise."

4) I said something brilliant in a meeting the other day. When a friend complimented me on my wisdom I reminded her that it was her idea. She had said it the meeting before. Now she had forgotten, but I remembered, so her voice carries on.

3) I asked my son, the one with the tattoo, earring, and orange hair, how life was coming with his roommates, and he said that it would be good if he could just get them to rinse their dishes before they put them into the sink. As I would say to him, "Goddamnittohell! Will you learn to rinse your dishes before you put them in the sink." As my father, back to the table, face to the darkening window, weary from the day testing meters, scrubbing with the worn steel wool would say to me, "Goddamnittohell! Will you learn to rinse your dishes before you put them in the sink."

2) One day with a ten-knot breeze from the south, the sails set for a beam reach and the autohelm doing the driving, I stood back

against the mast at ten degrees heel basking in the hills and sun of Lake Pepin. I sang to the universe, "Eloi, Eloi, lamma sabachthani?" which means, "My God, My God, why have you forsaken me?" for even in this moment when I had joined the eternal chorus I was aware and bitterly sad that it is not always like this.

1) As I drove the blue Toyota across the I-94 bridge with the commercial towers of the city rising to my right, I said to myself, "Great are the works of the Lord," and realized that with my blue suit, white shirt, and red tie, I was robed this morning to join the business choir. Sometimes I am tempted by my own insignificance not to come, and sometimes I am tempted by my own pride to claim an undeserved preeminence over other voices.

2) The cantor in a bored tone spoke dully the words, "Praise the Lord, I will extol the Lord with all my heart." My own heart opened and for a few moments I was not there but the spirit sang its praise of the creator through what used to be me. But of course, it was only a moment, and then I noticed the resonance of my own voice, and I was impressed by me so I had to come back. So perhaps the psalm should read, "My God, why have *I* forsaken *you?*" And the answer is that I find me so entrancing that I do not want to join the choir.

3) My wife had put on an audio tape made at a family Christmas party years before, and cutting under the sounds of my two boys rejoicing at their presents was my father's voice chanting out a constant hymn of comment, advice, and praise. "Now I would set that down if I were you, what could be in there, such a big boy to open it by himself, look what your brother has. . . ." On and on as was his wont with children irrespective of who was or was not listening or responding. Except since David was talking in full sentences my father was at least three years dead, so the voice I heard as my father's must have been mine. However, I am positive: Whoever was speaking, it was he.

4) In a business magazine the author of an essay referred to a friend of his who has a magnificent analogy for living out a career. That it is like tacking a sailboat up a channel, responding to the rise and fall, and the shifts in the wind. Since that is precisely

one of the chapters in my second book, I thought first that I should drop a nasty note requesting that he cease and desist. But then I thought what a compliment it was that another member of the choir had picked up my melody. And then I thought that perhaps he just had the same idea. It is not all that deep after all. And then I thought that maybe I read *his* book years ago and it was this, now forgotten, that gave me the idea for my chapter.

5) It is told that one spring morning, Father John, the Abbot of the monastery at Little River, went for a walk with Brother Jerome, the dishwasher. They were both ancient monks whose bladders brought them from bed well before the dawn. They returned to find that the gas main had blown, and the monastery with its seventy monks was gone. Father John asked Brother Jerome what he thought they should do, and Brother Jerome, a simple and insignificant man, looked at his watch and pointed out that it was time for choir. So Father John began, "O, Lord, open my lips" and Brother Jerome responded, "And my mouth shall announce your praise." Of course, neither of them meant a word of it, faced as they were with the loss of their home and the deaths of their brothers and companions.

But in heaven the archangel Michael sheathed his flaming sword and the archangel Gabriel laid down his dreadful trumpet and in hell Satan ceased his preparations, for the Lord had decreed that as long as the monastery at Little River prayed, Armageddon could not happen.

(Simple as this poetic description of non-dualistic life is, it parallels the dynamic monism of Alfred North Whitehead. What he terms an actual entity, an event on the molecular level, is in constant exchange with other actual entities, to the extent that their boundaries blur and the nexus among them takes on its own reality. I take heart from the parallel.)

9

Empty of Delusion

In the middle of the night
I go walking in my sleep
Through the jungle of doubt
To the river so deep
I know I am searching for something.

Something so undefined
That it could only be seen
By the eyes of the blind
In the middle of the night.

Billy Joel

Take Jesus Seriously

I swear to you, it is very difficult for the rich to enter heaven's domain, and again I tell you, it's easier for a camel to squeeze through a needle's eye than for a wealthy person to get into God's domain (17).

Explanation

The next chapters look at everything said before from two perspectives: "living empty" and "living now." These two ideas have been like porpoises accompanying a sailing ship, jumping and diving playfully just off the bow. At this point I wish to repeat nearly everything I have said before, but briefly, from these two perspectives. First, this chapter, which will describe everything said so far from the perspective of emptiness.

The Buddhist teacher waits for the moment of "no mind." She is waiting for the day when all of the noise shuts off and she is simply "observing." No delusions. That is a great day. It is a rare day. Of course, as all other days a passing day, except perhaps for a very blessed few people of whom Jesus was one.

In that set of moments reality itself will reach the consciousness. The experience of the Divine Presence, the great wholeness, along with the vivid outlines of every blade of grass appears before us. This way has been available the whole time.

"Whoever does not accept God's imperial rule the way a child would, certainly won't set foot in God's domain" (2).

A child is empty. There is nothing to bend reality. A child looks at life outside his or her own body and sees no concept because a concept is a memory of what has gone on before, a mushed up memory. One thousand three hundred and eighty two birds crammed into one concept, which is now imposed on any new bird. When a person can regularly and with ease create such a concept, he is no longer a child. He is an adult, and therefore never again shall he see a new bird, until, perhaps the adult learns to be empty as he was when he was a child. Free from delusion. Seeing what is there, nothing more, nothing less.

A child does not know that some feelings are good and some bad and some to be pursued and some to be escaped. A child is empty and allows what comes to come and what goes to go. Desires rise and fall without being captured in grim memory to be fulfilled or to be suffered about. Pain rises and falls to be forgotten as soon as it is absent, not to be feared until it happens. It is only what it is, not a memory of the past to be suffered repeatedly in the mind, or a memory of past pain projected into the future to fill the present with dread for what is not happening or may never happen.

A child is empty of cultural rules so does not know not to caress, not to belch, not to be thrilled at the enormous and successful movement of his own bowels. Therefore, a child lives all direct experiences directly.

A child is empty of the knowledge of who she is and enabled by this blessed ignorance is able to do whatever the body is capable of and the soul desires.

Some of the stories of Jesus indicate how the early Christians viewed the need for emptiness. When they made up a story about Jesus' birth, they did not give him royalty for parents. They gave him a peasant girl who said that God had chosen her because she was a nobody when deciding whom to make pregnant with his messenger. His father was a poor man and even then not really his father. He was born not in his parents' house but in a stable. What were they telling us, if not the necessity of being empty?

Meister Eckhart presents as the ideal an emptiness that allows the birth of God (the child) in the soul and then that presence prevents anything else from disturbing the emptiness: "Cast out all griefs so that perpetual joy reigns in your heart. Thus the child is born. And then if the child is born in me, the sight of father and all my friends slain before my eyes would leave my heart untouched. For if my heart were moved thereby, the child would not have been in me, though its birth might have been near."

Jesus said, "Congratulations, you poor. . . ." Luke says that Jesus turns to his disciples and says this. So he is congratulating them for choosing to be poor. The word for poor that he uses is not the word for those on the bottom of the economic scale, such as a person on welfare, but for someone off the charts, someone living under a bridge. He congratulates his disciples for they have left their families, professions, neighborhoods and chosen destitution for his name's sake.

Those who have chosen to be poor are empty, and their emptiness will be filled. They have forfeited their own lives, and therefore a new life will be given to them. They are the passersby who take what comes along the path because they are empty of investment in what should be there.

Paul says: "Therefore I am content with weakness, with mistreatment, with distress, with persecutions and difficulties for the sake of Christ; for when I am powerless, it is then that I am strong." A moment earlier he had said that the Lord said: "My grace is enough for you, for in weakness power reaches perfection" (2 Cor).

Jesus had compassion for the rich because they are not empty. "I swear to you, it is very difficult for the rich to enter heaven's domain, and again I tell you, it's easier for a camel to squeeze through a needle's eye than for a wealthy person to get into God's domain" (17).

I find this a painful text. I am wealthy. Almost any citizen of the United States is wealthy. Living at our poverty level provides more of the world's goods than middle income does in most of the world. But even beyond that I am wealthy. Is Jesus saying that it will be difficult for me to enter the kingdom of heaven?

Most certainly!

The problem is not the wealth itself but the attitude, skills, and knowledge required to generate the wealth. The wealthy are filled with competence. We know what to do and how to do it. We have connections. We are self-sufficient. We are not empty.

In this set of people terminal cancer is an opportunity to mobilize all these resources in the battle to fight it to the end. "We know the most famous oncologist at Mayo." "We can fly the patient to Germany for the latest treatment at the most successful laboratory." "We will organize prayer groups that will pray so hard that he is bound to recover."

At the end, usually, the same answer comes to the rich person as to the poor person. The rich person's very bravery and confidence in self-sufficiency is sad.

He and she and I are full of dreams and calculations, and schemes and standards. When we try to be good people, when we try to enter the kingdom, our hearts and minds are too full and our attitude is too oriented towards being successful. We scheme, plot, and plan on how to enter the kingdom successfully. This is precisely the wrong way to go.

It is we who ask the Dalai Lama to teach us the fast way to successful kingdom finding. Weep with us, for we are poorer than the poor are. Trapped in our own success and trapped in the paradigm of seeking success we cannot find it. Meditation practice becomes one more skill to develop in pursuit of the excellent life. Squeeze it in between racquetball, picking up the kids, making the sale, and super sex. List it with all the rest of my skills.

Fredrick Buechner in *The Sacred Journey* says:

> You can survive on your own. You can grow strong on your own. You can even prevail on your own. But you cannot become human on your own. Surely that is why, in Jesus' sad joke, the rich man has as hard a time getting into Paradise as that camel through the needle's eye because with his credit card in his pocket, the rich man is so effective at getting for himself everything he needs that he does not see that what he needs more than anything else in the world can be had only as a gift.

It is the poor who are given the head start in becoming aware of the kingdom. Those who know they can't make it on their own because they have not made it in the past. It is the poor who are the good ground for the spiritual life because they know they need something, and they turn to its promise with empty hearts. It is the poor who find it easier to say, "Thy will be done."

I have seen poor wealthy people. As Jesus said, it is not likely, but it is a lovely sight when it happens. I have been a consultant to chief executive officers that listen, raconteurs who love to hear a story, running backs that brag about the linemen who block for them. I know leaders who serve. They are there. Poor wealthy people are there because we *can* choose. It is difficult, but we *can* choose.

I once asked my parishioner, the mayor of a wealthy suburb, what he thought when he drove among its lakes and saw the poor from the inner city clustered on the well manicured banks fishing, their rattletrap cars parked bunched up under the ancient elms. He said, "I think 'Maybe we need more public docks and more public parking.'" In the midst of Christianity, I encountered a Christian. Why should I be surprised?

On the other hand, I have seen wealthy poor people. People with little who become bitter under the burdens. They desire what they cannot have. Poverty is no guarantee of perfection. It is easier in a culture where few have anything and the poor can go about living in the glory of what is available to them: family, friends, community, flowers, time. In our culture what the poor do not have is waved in front of them daily by their neighbors and by the culture. It becomes difficult to be content.

No matter what our wealth and even more no matter what our talents on the day of our baptism, we declared ourselves empty. We gave up the delusion that we can do this ourselves. We went under the water full, and we died there, and empty of our old life we rose from the water, as a person rises from the dead, expecting the Divine Presence to fill us with a new life. To the extent that we were empty, that is what happened and what will continue to happen.

We have a choice. It is not an easy choice. But we have a choice. Indeed, the poor to whom Jesus addressed the sentence "Blessed are you poor. . . ." were people who had made the choice to be poor. They had had jobs, and now that they followed him they were beggars. They were skillful, and now they were dependent. They were respected citizens, and now they were outcasts. Their lives had had cultural meaning, and now they followed a bizarre crazy man who fit nowhere.

Sometimes life helps even those of us who are rich. One advantage to being a consultant is that I got fired more often than most people, and with less devastating consequences because when one client fired me, others did not, at least not at the same moment. The more violent of these firings were often the ones that I learned the most from, once I had emptied myself of the anger and certitude that I was right and they were wrong.

I remember the heart palpitations and cold sweat that went with the awareness that I was not potent enough to control my own future and that others saw me differently than my projected image. The basic fear was not that I had been fired, or dumped, or rejected. The basic fear was realizing that my narcissistic image of myself as permanent self-sufficiency was flawed to its very core. (Illness also teaches this lesson.)

The baptism of Jesus in the Jordan was the culminating point when he emptied himself, and the Spirit of God took him over. Jesus of Nazareth emptied himself in an extraordinary way and into that emptiness the Spirit of God rushed. When the Divine Presence takes on flesh this is what it looks like. That little boy of Nazareth was no longer there, and God's Spirit now controlled this flesh. His person was washed away. He was transparent. Consciousness as a whole was able to work through him.

The Jesus Seminar is certain that he healed people. (That from a bunch of skeptical liberals.) He was consciousness whole and entire touching consciousness ill or injured.

All that stands between us and being Jesus clones is our willingness to be empty. That is quite a bit. So we meditate. We look at what is there with loving attention, and we see our fullness. As we watch it, it dissipates, and emptiness appears.

Through this practice I am less full than I once was. There may be a faster course, a more thorough method, a more dramatic way, but this is all I know, so I practice it. At least now I am not hung up forever in what the Buddhists call "monkey mind." At least now from time to time I grow rather quiet inside. At least now, I leave some cracks for the Spirit to slip in, some moments to be aware of the magnificence that is the Divine Presence in me.

Sometimes I feel a new breath in my very center calling me to new directions. The emptiness brought on by meditation allows me to hear the Spirit's voice buried there. "Father, we thank thee who has planted, thy name in our hearts." the hymn peals.

This same emptiness in a much more ordinary way allows the Spirit's voice to speak to me through Scripture. I find that I now understand it more clearly. I find it calling my heart more strongly. I find the practice of meditation allows me to quietly look and see what is there. The psalms, those visceral prayer poems from thousands of years ago, now spring off the page at me with a new life.

The ebbing of my need to maintain the delusion that I am John allows me to hear the Spirit in the voices of others. I am more ready to think over an unpleasant message, willing to mull over my enemy's words, chewing them for the truth that God has slipped between his accusations or threats.

I now look more carefully at what I once would have simply called outdated practices or theories from my mother the Church and see that while part of what is being said will not withstand the light of a modern mind, still in the core somewhere lurks the truth that my grandparents sensed.

UU (THE BOTTOM LINE)

A different life becomes more available the more I can be empty. Life in the kingdom is available only to those who think like a child empty of the delusions of an adult. "I swear to you, it is very difficult for the rich to enter heaven's domain, and again I tell you, it's easier for a camel to squeeze through a needle's eye than for a wealthy person to get into God's domain" (17).

Practical Matters

When sitting, pay attention to your scheming and planning. You are trying to control the future with your competence. This is the rich person coming out in you. Life demands a certain level of planning, but normally the fact that you are doing this during meditation is a clear indicator that you are not empty. Be alert to the fact that your planning and scheming is a symptom of an idiot at a deeper level. This idiot thinks you should be in charge, not God. Level your gentle and loving gaze upon him. Perhaps he may grow quieter and even from time to time, desist.

Walking Meditation

Another way to meditate is "walking meditation." In the forms of this I have found comfortable, we no longer focus on the breath but focus on the legs.

Pick an eight-foot path, more or less. You will be going up and down this path. While there are merits to just walking somewhere, as soon as you do that, you begin to focus not on the walking, but on the goal you are aiming at as your destination. Back and forth removes the delusion of progress. Walk at whatever speed enables you to pay attention. Usually that means slower than a normal walk. That is what I do, with my focus sometimes on the knees, sometimes on the ankles, often on the way the feet feel touching the ground or floor. (Bare or stocking feet helps this by providing a definite tactile response.)

Some people walk very slowly indeed. Noticing the heel lifting, and now the toes leaving the floor, and now the foot moving, and now the heel touching the floor, and now the toes touching the floor, and repeat. Do whatever helps your concentration.

Hands are usually folded on the tummy, one hand in a fist gripping the thumb of the other hand, the other hand's fingers resting on the back of the first hand.

Try walking meditation from time to time. I usually use it as a break from sitting meditation.

Questions and Answers

1) Q: I am still confused about the difference between dualism and non-dualism.

A: As we speak of such things as the differences between dualism and non-dualism, my greatest fear is that we shall forget to sit.

The masters are perfectly clear that the road to whatever is out there is through awareness of the material, most particularly, awareness of my own body. I get sucked out into a world of ideas and lose track of the fact of my body. If I can learn to focus my awareness on my body, live as "awareness in a body," then I learn that feelings and thoughts and relationships are all "things in the body." As such these delusions have less power to influence my well being than the pragmatic happiness of the body. I prefer to focus on the glory of the day striking my eye and release the tension in my shoulders resulting from tomorrow's work still undone, of course.

This is immediate tranquility immediately available. It may lead somewhere else, but if I focus on getting somewhere else all of this will disappear in a flicker. That is why the masters send us back to sit when we start floating around in our heads or out of our heads too much.

If you don't understand the difference between dualism and non-dualism at this point, don't worry about it. I am not sure I do.

2) Q: Is there a connection among "emptiness," such practices as "Lenten penance" and "will power?"

A: It depends who was teaching the last two to you. Some of my grade school religion teachers had at best limited understanding of what they were about. They might say that it helps Jesus to have you hurt yourself and offer up your pain. However, I think some of them had a pretty good grasp of the way it works. One of those would say: "Through Lenten penance you learn that you can separate yourself from your desire for some perfectly good thing. By separating yourself from one thing, you can learn to separate yourself from all your desires. With that separation comes the ability to choose what you want and stick to it unmoved by your desires." One Buddhist master says that our feelings are like an elephant in rut and that it is mindfulness (loving attention) that is the post that keeps them from going berserk.

This looks like "will power" but is not really anything about a powerful will. I now get credit for will power at a party because I don't accept a whisky and water as I come through the door. But I am not exercising my will. I am just aware that my desire for whisky and water is weak, and both it and my desire to do the social thing exist in a different room from the empty one from which I make my decisions. I exert no effort here.

3) Q: Where does childhood end? It seems to end so much sooner than we would think these days. Hovering on the edge of six, my son is close to no longer seeing the magical, trusting the raw sensations and emotions caused by a new object or event. My eight-year-old daughter left this place even sooner. Even at four and a half she no longer saw the magic. It is hard for me to grasp "the becoming as a child" when I cannot even remember ever seeing that way. I have no conscious memory of seeing things in this pure sense. It seems as if my judgments came with me from my mother's womb, and for all her troubles in life, I believe that may be the case.

A: I agree with you that children now are growing up very quickly and that this does indeed interfere with their opportunity to live in a preconceptual world. However, I think perhaps you have had preconceptual moments. They are characterized by "wonder." When you feel "wonder" odds are that you are staring something in its preconceptual face. You see a sunset, instead of the concept of sunsets, and you feel wonder.

4) Q: When I paddle my kayak, sometimes I experience a definite shift in my perspective. Everything becomes peaceful and quiet. Extraordinarily beautiful is how I would describe it. I came to this class hoping to recreate this feeling, and so far it has not happened.

A: What I am about to say is really too important to be buried here in the Q & A, but since this is the way it has come up this is the way I will present it.

Early in this process we focused on seeing without concept. Let the bird be a bird and empty myself of the concept of birdness that stands between the observing the bird and me. The final emptiness is to empty myself of the concept that is me. Get rid of "John" since he is a delusion. When I empty myself of the concept of a bird, I then see a real bird. But when I empty myself of the concept of "John," there is nothing left to see. In order to see John I looked back into myself and created the concept of John out of the pieces. Empty of the concept, I now can only look outward. While aware of what is passing through I have no organizing principle to explain what is occurring.

I am then in the non-state of no-mind. I am aware of impulses that simply pass through this empty space and explode into action. As one student has expressed it: "It is like you were an announcer describing yourself playing baseball, and the announcer disappears, and there you are in the middle of the game with no words being said about it. Everything becomes action." Or as another student expressed it, "Everything became very clear, and I became a dotted line."

This non-state in itself is not the same as being aware of the Divine Presence, but it is one way to prepare the ground for that awareness. It is called a "non-state" because the word "state" is reserved for a consistent immersion in a particular pattern of delusion. This is not delusion.

I leave this critical fact buried here for a number of reasons:

First, I realized its necessity because of your question, and the question itself raises issues that should be seen as this is glimpsed.

Second, just as you accidentally tripped into this place while kayaking, many people are tripped while doing many things, all things that get them to forget themselves. I suspect that this is what occurs to some of our youth at a rock concert. They get emptied of themselves.

Third, effort will not get you here. Accident will, but you cannot work at that. However, awareness will. Particularly awareness of yourself creating the concept of yourself. Awareness of mind leads to no-mind. This has been what we have been about since chapter two.

Fourth, most people are not likely to experience no-mind. Most people sitting in meditation experience less-mind. This quiet emptying is wonderful in itself but no match for the quiet and beauty of no-mind. The first is a difference of the degree of noise. The second is the absence of noise.

You have set yourself a magnificent intention. Effort will not help. Simply be aware of your mind, particularly that mind that creates a sense of person, with the hope that observing it with loving awareness will cause it to shut off.

5) Q: Could you say some more about the observer. I experience the observer as the first step in the process and the key to everything else.

A: The observer is not the first step. I speak of it as that in the early part of the book because it is easier to experience than what I say next. If you are extremely attentive, you will become aware of "observing" as the first step, not "observer." When you observe the observer who is observing? (The question echoes the Zen questions: "What is your original face? Who are you before 'yes' and 'no'?") This game could be played *ad infinitum*. The way out of the conundrum is the awareness of observing without a subject. This is the experience of "no-mind." This is the sound of one hand clapping. See answer above.

6) Q: I try in meditation to become aware of myself as connected to everything else, and I just cannot do it.

A: Please don't try. Everybody who has told me of having the experience of universal oneness, and I have heard from at least a dozen people over the years, has had it by accident. Often they cannot even tell what the accident was that brought it about. The "causes" I have heard sound as varied as for one a moment of tranquility, for another a sense of hopelessness, for another a crowded brain. Even more, I have seen no evidence that the experience was anything but a passing phenomenon that had little effect on their lives or happiness long term. (Although it did create a certainty about the delusion of normal life that was inescapable.)

On the other hand, waking up to the present reality will effect your daily life. Just try bit by bit to be aware, and you will get there.

To be more precise, while I have not met people who live in unity I have no doubt that they exist. Just not functioning out here. I read of a Hindu yogi who kept having the experience of unity. He was a postal worker in India. He got his physician to declare him disabled by bliss so that he could receive disability pay and retire to a hermitage. If you really lived in this bliss you would become non-functional in this world of dualism, not an alarming possibility I suppose but not one that I seek. But I have no doubt that tucked here and there throughout the world are some former postal workers smiling deeply at the reality they see that I cannot.

I look on the fact of our deep interconnectedness much as I look on the fact taught me by physics that what appears solid material as this chair in which I am sitting is really energy. It is interesting. I will take it into account. But I still will trust the chair to hold me up.

I am cautious about harming others since we are really not two, but in the morning "I" get up and go to work to earn "my" salary, to eat "my" food, to have "my" house. Dualism is not the underlying reality, but things work that way for the most part. If I run a stop light, the cop will give me a ticket even if I explain to him that I am the interconnection of multiple forces and not a person at all and therefore not responsible. If I annoy him enough, his delusion may put my delusion in the squad car to transport it to a place where it may rest awhile. Since I do not want some psychiatrist asking me pointed questions in the lockup ward, I try to play it cool in normal life. I am a little afraid of what he or she might make of my answers.

One day while visiting a church in another city, the rector asked me who I was. Deeply influenced by the Taize service she had just led I answered, "A slice of the Divine." If she was not ready for this, and I assure you she wasn't, neither are most people.

Here is an explanation for the experience of being one with the universe. Some students of the brain think that what happens is that in deep meditation the part of the brain that tells you what is you and what is not you behaves differently. You lose your sense of separation. I am one who thinks that doing this simply introduces the doer to an unreal state. (Drugs can effect that same brain function.) We are really trapped in our bodies and must become aware of that. Our freedom comes in realizing our participation in the flow.

Others think that this sense of oneness is to be sought and that it is the ultimate reality. They outnumber my little group and have better credentials than I. Indeed, my stance may simply be sour grapes that I do not live in bliss, but one reason I do not is that I think it a bad idea.

7) Q: This then brings me to something like predestination. All the forces add up and then I do what I do. Am I responsible for my behavior?

A: Doesn't look that way does it? The Buddhist answer is that you must act as if you were responsible for the good order of society. Or to pop back to the previous answer, things work as if I were responsible. Responsibility is one of the forces, and if I avoid that force things will come out differently. As you noted in class we could come to the same problem down a Christian path. If God knows everything and is all-powerful, then is not the game over? One answer is we must act as if it is not because that is part of the game. (Another answer, as noted elsewhere, is that God is not all-powerful.)

8) Q: The fact that Jesus uses the word "hate" for what I am to do with my relatives seems too strong to me. Could this be an incorrect translation?

A: The Jesus scholars do not think so. However, as I have described above, it is not the people themselves that are being hated but the social roles implied by the words "mother," "father, "etc. The quote from the *Five Gospels* on Luke 14:26 is that

> the severity of this saying can only be understood in the context of the primacy of filial relationships. Individuals had no real existence apart from their ties to blood relatives, especially parents. If one did not belong to a family, one had no real social existence. Jesus is therefore confronting the social structures that governed his society at their core. For Jesus, family ties faded into insignificance in relation to God's imperial rule, which he regarded as the fundamental claim on human loyalty.

If you are having trouble understanding the term "social existence," all you must do is pay attention the next time strangers gather in your presence. They will tell each other where they came from, who their relatives are, what they do for a living and many other boring details in an effort to establish their "social existence." Assuming you are somewhat normal, you are probably doing the same thing. Ask yourself "why?" Bereft of that social existence, your real existence has a chance to rise to your awareness.

This takes us a step beyond what the Jesus scholars saw in the quote from Jesus. I am no longer simply speaking of where I focus my attention, but now I am talking about who I am.

Am I the product of social mirrors, or am I a child of God? Can you feel the shift of energy and the freedom as you turn from being the former and become the latter?

9) Q: Are not forgiveness and compassion forms of emptiness?

A: Well said. Since you are reluctant to say more let me expound. In both forgiveness and compassion I am empty of a standard for judging behavior. Behavior, mine or another person's, just is. No concept of what it should be. In "T" group methodology I was encouraged not to judge the other person's behavior. How would they ever change? I was urged to report the effects of their behavior on me.

So in the example your wife just used, she is no longer applying a standard to her daughter-in-law's behavior and judging her wrong. Some day it might be helpful to say to her, "The way you are always focusing on minutiae I find very annoying." Of course, that raises the possibility your wife may hear back how her daughter-in-law feels about a life lived ignoring details. But this at least gets them both in the real world. What is this right and wrong? Life is much more free and empty when it is reaction to each other.

This way of looking at life is also helpful in looking at self. I get angry often. But why mess up my mind by applying the standard derived from some other people for what is the proper level of anger? If I keep the mind empty, then I can look at the effects in the world of my anger and the effects in me. Then I can decide if I would like more of this anger, less of this anger, or more judicious application of this anger.

So in forgiveness and compassion my mind is empty of a standard. It is also empty of the energy required to hold the world to the standard and of all the accompanying internal and sometimes external rhetoric involved in justifying the standard and explaining the depth of the offense against the standard. Thus the mind gets quieter quickly.

10

"Now" as Reality, "Past" and "Future" as Delusion

From all sides, then, our present is bounded and sand-wiched between past and future. It is limited, fenced, restricted. It is not an open moment: it is a squeezed moment, a pressed moment, and therefore a fleeting moment. It just passes. Since the past and the future seem so real, our present moment, the very meat of the sandwich, is reduced to a mere thin slice, so that our reality soon becomes all bread-ends with no filling.

Ken Wilbur

Take Jesus Seriously

Right then and there they abandoned their nets and followed him (3).

Explanation

If we do what Jesus suggests the effect will be that we will live in the "now." When Jesus talks about living the will of the Father without anxiety, he is talking about living "now." The concept of "now" living is clearer in Buddhism and very clear in the humanistic psychology of our day.

Let's run back through the ideas presented to this point and see how thinking of them as they relate to the "now" will give us a method for instantly checking if our attitude is the attitude that Jesus taught.

Chapter 2: The Practice of Meditation

We can only be aware of one thing at a time. Most people most of the time try to be aware of several things at once and therefore are really aware of none of them. According to Gestalt psychology what we are aware of is a figure that has emerged from a background. We see our spouse's face, and the kitchen wall is in the background. If we focus on the wall, it becomes figure, and our spouse's face turns into background. If we try to be aware of the cereal we are eating, the cigarette we are smoking, the newspaper we are reading, the kitchen wall surrounding us, and our spouse's face, we are aware of none of them. They all become background. A figure does not emerge.

In this practice we learn that we can only bring one object at a time into the moment. We are aware of our breath. Worry about tomorrow tugs at our mind. We know we cannot be aware of two things. The worry keeps tugging. We come aware of ourselves as worrying. While not immersing ourselves in the worrying process (immersion is another manner of not being aware), we do give the fact that we are worrying full attention. We even label it "worrying" to insure that we are really noticing it fully. When it disappears, we look for the breath and wait for whatever will next request our concentration.

I know that in any given "now" I can only be aware of one thing. This practice teaches me to focus on that which is emerging.

Chapter 3: Material Reality

We put concepts between material reality and ourselves. No longer do we see a fluttering piece of glory, or a tired but caring woman, or a shy man, but we see a "bird" and a "mother" and a "Senior-Vice-President of Research and Development."

Where did the concept come from? From the past! We have assembled our past encounters with the thing itself, and then our past encounters with various concepts of the thing itself, until we have in this moment not the thing itself but our past memories of it mushed into a concept. This we have called a delusion. It is not the material reality. We have invented it.

To leap from the attitude in which we tend to view reality to the attitude that Jesus taught we simply ask ourself: "What is present before me *now*?" If I can see what is there now, I will see without concept or delusion the reign of God extended before me. How do I experience my body *now*? The question pulls me back into the reality of being "awareness in a body."

As I sit in meditation, I experience only the sounds, sights, and sensations present to me now. My constant touchstone for what I wish to have in my consciousness is what is happening now. Not the memory of yesterday's beach or the daydream of to-morrow's motorcycle ride, but the sights, smells, sounds and sensations of this room and this body now.

I am practicing loving attention. Devoid of the past, not expecting the future, all that I have is my attention, and I apply my attention bare of concept to the object before me. At this point I am living where Jesus taught me to live.

Chapter 4: Feelings and Thoughts

What creates all those thoughts and feelings that keep rattling through my head, disturbing my quiet, and confusing me as to who I really am in this moment? Remembering the past and manipulating the future are the sources of this noise.

Thoughts and feelings arise to repeat the pleasure that once was there. A cardboard pleasure based on a past that no longer exists stands between me and the real pleasures available now.

Thoughts and feelings arise to regret the errors I once made. Worthless tears being shed may block me from rising to the responsibilities of the present.

The past is not here. It is over. These are remnants. As remnants they have no power, and they will fade away into a blessed silence.

My feelings and thoughts arise in part to cope with the future. I am planning and scheming to make sure it goes well. These mental tasks are powered by the anxiety for the future that Jesus says we should hand over to the Father. If I can let the future be and live in the "now," schemes and planning will have no necessity, and they will fade away into a blessed silence.

As I sit in meditation my constant touchstone is: Is this that is running through my head a product of "now," or is it a memory or a scheme. Labeling I add to what is happening the word past or future. "Future planning." "Past remembering." I watch them for they are what is there, but with the label I am more likely to pay attention fully and then to return to the breath and other present sensations, providing them my loving attention, and allow the delusions of past and future to dissolve.

Chapter 5: Desire

Desire is the "now's" absolute enemy. Why do I not see the glory of "now"? Why am I not living in the kingdom? I do not see it because I refuse to live now. Indeed as a person on this particular way, it is my desire to be in the kingdom that blocks me from being in the kingdom. I would like it to arrive tomorrow and therefore cannot see that it must arrive today.

> The kingdom
> Is scheduled to arrive
> "Now"

I am like a person standing on a bus stop looking for the bus down the street while the bus is waiting next to me. If I wake up to living in the "now," desire will cease, for there is nothing to be desired, it is all now.

In meditation when I experience restlessness, I ask myself, "Are you trying to escape this moment in favor of a better one?" And then I remind myself that the kingdom is found now, not in the future.

I have moments of clear awareness that the one thing preventing me from realizing the presence of God is a daydream of the future that encapsulates and plays out one of my little desires. I cannot tell you what prevents me from setting aside the dream of the future in favor of living in the divine presence other than fear of a new form of life.

Chapter 6: The Reality of Pain

The price tag for avoiding pain is to leave the "now." When pain happens it happens. The only way to avoid it is to mentally go somewhere else and sometime else. The kingdom includes pain. The memory of pain is buried in our soma and will stay there infecting all "nows" with unawareness until it is brought into the aware "now" and wept over. To ask myself "Am I avoiding pain or buried pain now?" and then facing what comes up brings us into the kingdom.

Indeed at the deepest level it is an unwillingness to live even with the nuisance of this body that takes me out of the now. I refuse to be content with what this place and moment have to offer. I am tempted to scheme and daydream about other and better situations. Coming into the now involves acceptance of the limitations of body. I cannot ignore the climb up the stairs to supper as a drag placed on spirit by my body, but I must learn to accept the knees bending and lifting weight as one of the pleasures of the day because it is all that I have in that very moment.

Chapter 7: The Delusion of Permanence

If I experience the now I will experience it as passing. The now flows. Because I am afraid of impermanence I pretend that all nows are alike. I pretend that nothing is moving. Attention to the now will wake me up to the flow of life.

Chapter 8: The Delusion of Person

The teacher who brought Buddhism from India to China was asked by the emperor, "Who are you?" He answered that he did not know.

When we say we know who we are, what we are saying is that we know who we have been and we intend to hold that constellation of characteristics together for the rest of time. If a person did not define self in terms of the past, and did not intend to hold/create a particular self in the future, that person would not know who they are about to become, and since all instants are past as they reach consciousness, would not know who they are. I am just a dot waiting right "now" for the Spirit to define the future. It is in that understanding that the early Christians learned not to plan what they said but to trust that the Spirit would move them when the time came.

Chapter 9: Empty

Does your head often feel crowded? The experience of many meditation practitioners is that the head often feels spacious. The mind feels if there is room in there for much more. What has happened? It is past memory and future schemes that crowd the head. I am trying to focus on everything at once. If I can focus on one thing and leave the rest in the background, I find extra room in the mind's house.

Why do I not experience the Spirit of God? I do not experience the Spirit because I am full of the past and future. Why does not the question of what it means to exist force itself onto my consciousness? There is no room because my consciousness is already occupied with the past and the future. Why am I unaware of the presence of the Ground of all being? Because the sunlight of my awareness falls on past and future, leaving the Divine Presence in the shadow.

In meditation, and of course in life, if I can just live in the "now," room will be left for the Spirit. I do not need to seek the Divine Presence. If I can provide empty space, the Divine Presence will become obvious.

The story is told of Jesus curing a blind man, Bartimaeus (19). When Bartimaeus realizes that it is Jesus that is walking by, he calls out to him, loudly. The disciples try to get him to be quiet, but he will not be quiet. Jesus hears him and has him brought over. Looking at Bartimaeus, obviously blind, Jesus asks him: "What do you want?"

Is that not surprising? What would a blind man want if confronting a famous healer? Bartimaeus tells him that he wants to see again. And Jesus cures him on the spot. But sometimes blind people do not want to be cured. In our day many of the existentially blind do not even know that they are blind.

I see myself as a blind man who until quite recently has not wanted to admit he is blind. So as Jesus passes by, and he does daily in the Scriptures I read, in the conversations I have, and in the thoughts running through my head, I do not call out to him. I have been fine.

Frequently he has asked me what I would have from life, and since I did not know that I was blind, I answered him that I would like a motorcycle, or a better job, or health for my children. I asked him for many things but not for sight.

Finally, I realize that I am blind, and now he asks me what I want, and I say tomorrow I would like to see. Today I would like a motorcycle, or a better job, or health for my children.

So he passes by, and I still do not see.

> The reign of God
> Is happening
> Now.

Once upon a time Jesus passed a bunch of really busy people, successful businessmen in the fishing industry, suppliers of other peoples' suppers, and devoted family men supporting wives and children. Jesus asked them to follow him. As far as we know, not one of them requested a rain check. The call came and they responded now. "Right then and there they abandoned their nets and followed him" (3). Jesus viewed people who tried to delay for even the best of reasons as living in a fashion inimical to the reign of God. "First, let me go and bury my father" (3) gained the man saying it not approval but sudden disbarment from the band of disciples. In effect Jesus said, "That's was it, buddy, you missed the call. We live now. Not after we bury our fathers."

UU (THE BOTTOM LINE)

A simple way to bring to the forefront all of these lessons is to focus on living in the present moment.

Practical Matters

Consider adding to your meditation practice "meditative eating." Just paying attention to your eating. Slow down. Make a decision of what to put in your mouth next. Consider it. Cut it. Consider it. Stab it. Consider it. Lift it. Consider it. Place it in your mouth. Taste it. Chew it slowly. Notice how the taste shifts. Pay attention to your swallow. Privacy usually helps for this. It takes forever to eat a meal this way, and you look "funny" to others. However, even in a restaurant with friends at the table when I feel like I am being carried out of life awareness, a couple of bites like this bring me back to the table without anyone being the wiser.

If the pork chop is going to cost me $19.95, it deserves at least my loving attention.

"Now" and Eating Meditation

I find that eating meditation is an excellent method for becoming aware of how little time I spend in the "now." I just finished a lunch of egg roll, rice, two buttered rice cakes, and two dessert rice cakes. I practiced Eating Meditation.

As I ate rice I looked forward to the egg roll. As I moved my fork to the egg roll, I considered how good a buttered rice cake could taste. As I chewed on the buttered rice cake, I looked forward to the desert rice cake. Through all of this, I drafted the words I am writing "now." I perhaps spent two minutes out of twenty paying any attention to what I was eating at that very moment.

At the start of the meal, to my left was a huge cup of tea. At the end of the meal, the cup was empty.

Do you suppose I drank it?

The Now and Conversation

The disciples were told that they should not worry about what they were to say but rely on the Spirit. Avoid planning conversations before you have them. Planning is a way of avoiding the now and avoiding the Spirit both in you and in the other. During the conversation speak succinctly, and then watch the other person for response. Do not try to steer his or her response by what you say. Say what you say. Observe with loving attention what they say. Then respond to it. Conversations will become Sprit filled and exciting.

Questions and Answers

1) Q: How did it happen—that feeling of your connection to the Divine Presence? Do you sometimes have feelings of rage and hate? If you do what do you do with them?

   A: My feeling of connection to the Divine Presence may have to do more with how fuzzy my picture is of the Divine Presence than anything else. I sense a movement of consciousness throughout history that matches up with my own experience of consciousness. So not like I believe in some guy up there watching out for me. On the other hand, the word "consciousness" is too weak to depict the feeling of intention and purposefulness that I experience.

   I frequently feel rage and hate. Usually I just vent to wife and friends. Sometimes I shout at the person who has me angry. Sometimes I confront them. It usually takes me quite a while to make it to loving attention to the feeling. Sometimes it takes a month. Usually the feelings that are difficult to face have to do with desires that are important to me, particularly protecting my delusions about who I am as a person. When you asked this question, did you think I was someone special? Don't look for the Buddha over here. (Or maybe I am not so bad. Both the Buddha and Jesus wept in the presence of tragedy.)

If the question really meant, "What should one do?" then the answer is to sit with the feelings, trying always to see where they are occurring in the body. Sometimes in that process their source becomes clearer, so one can move from anger to realizing that the issue is that I have been hurt, or that my ego is affronted, or my sense of competence challenged. Once one becomes aware of how the body and the spirit are ravaged by such feelings, the feelings tend to pass in self-protection. They are distasteful.

2) Q: I tried looking at things that came up during meditation and just emptying myself of them. As I set various roles and feelings outside of myself, room and quiet grew inside me.

A: This sounds like a great exercise to be done from time to time. The thing to watch out for is that "you" are deciding, and desiring, and putting. "You" decide what should go outside. "You" desire that it go outside. "You" put it outside. I suggest on a normal basis observing what comes up. It will go away if it should. I repeat "on a normal basis" because the exercise you did should be helpful and sounds like it was. The problem with it is that the "you" who is doing all that has to find the door and exit too. It's the boss idiot.

3) Q: I want to understand this in terms of human relationships too. I find so often that my relationships with others get off track—I cannot leave behind past wrongs, and I fear future wrongs. Is this not useful? Does it not protect a person from being hurt by a person known to be hurtful? This is certainly the premise on which our overcrowded prison system is based.

Then I think of Jesus and how often he admonishes us to forgive our brother. Is this considered to be an actual Jesus statement by the Jesus scholars? Forgive people seven times seventy times.

A: Certainly there is wisdom in avoiding being hurt again. The things to balance with this legitimate concern are: First, to what extent do I have to stop being a full human being to avoid the risk of this person or people in general hurting me. Second, to what extent does the "hurt" that I refer to here really hurt? Is it broken bones or hard looks?

The seven times seventy quote seems not to be from Jesus; however, there are at least two quotes that are from him that are equally strong. "Forgive and you'll be forgiven." "Father, forgive our debts to the extent we have forgiven others" (7). Note the intimate connection between forgiving and being forgiven. Leaving aside dualistic language, when you hold on to past wrongs and fear future wrongs the universe in its immediate representative, you, takes on a twisted painful approach to life. Life becomes indirect to the point of pain. Leaving that aside makes possible a direct and radiant approach to life.

Gandhi was warned by friends that the British Governor of India would take advantage of Gandhi's straightforwardness and do him harm. Gandhi replied that that is what happens to people like him. But he was unwilling to take on the pain of a shrewd existence simply to avoid the pain of suffering the governor's treachery.

4) Q: You say you are different from most Christians teaching meditation in that you encourage people to observe the reality that is there and other teachers try to establish a reality by saying a prayer or doing a reading, but you have chapter after chapter about what is supposed to be there. In short, are you not encouraging us to become empty, distance ourselves from our thoughts and feelings, deny the reality of our person, as just three examples of the state you want us to create?

A: No, I am not doing that. Or at least I should not be doing that. Now I am going to have to go through the whole manuscript and make sure that I am not doing that because I am a little suspicious that I may have been some of the time doing precisely that.

What I should be saying is that if you observe with loving attention what is happening this is what I suspect you will see happening based on my experience and the experience of my teachers. If you observe your thoughts and feelings, you will see that they are not you, just wandering through. If you observe your person, you will see that it is something you are making up. If you observe all the stuff that is rushing around, it will show itself as chimera and will dissolve leaving you empty.

As you first begin this practice, all that is charging around inside you may create an indefinable shadowy chaos. At my best I am saying to you: "Here are some descriptions of what might be going on. Is that what is happening? Maybe that shadow is "desire." Maybe this one "fears of impermanence." Maybe this one "defense of your sense of person."

Your question illuminates for me my need to be preachy instead of scientific. Perhaps if I observe my need to be preachy, it will go away?

5) Q: So then what is "reality?" How do you define it?

A: I am not able to define it. May I point you to Alfred North Whitehead's *Process and Reality*? The answer to that question requires more philosophical understanding than I have even after reading him, but what I can do is tell you what I mean by "being aware of reality." By that I mean being aware of my own sensations. I experience sensations in the body, pain, warmth, tension, tickle, and itch. I experience perceptions in the body, seeing, smelling, hearing, touching. I experience emotions in my body, anger, lust, love, caring, fear. I experience thoughts in my body, worrying, planning, daydreaming. That which I am absolutely sure of is that I experience these sensations as sensations. I am not sure that there is an object outside of my body deserving my feelings. I am not even confident of the nature of what I perceive. I know I experience the sensation of "red." But is what I see as "red," the same as what others report as "red"? I am less sure.

Quite probably the universe I think I see outside of my body is fairly real also. Some take this to the point of denying that reality, but I do not. However, ask me what I call reality with confidence; it is my sensations.

In normal life most ignore their sensations in favor of accepting the reality of that which is sensed. In this practice we are trying to be aware of the sensations themselves. This awareness will lead to clarity and brightness.

6) Q: You speak of the person as a construct, but I am pretty sure that in meditation I experience myself as a discrete entity, different than others.

   A: If we took a snapshot of you and I at a given moment, we would see that we are discrete entities. But that is because we took a snapshot. Life is in flow. Both of us change from moment to moment and change and are changed by those around us. I am more I than I am you because this body has a history separate from yours. But the longer we engage in conversation, the more I become connected to you. That is why a student in your group was able to meditate for her husband. The more she meditates, the more her husband is affected by being close to one who meditates.

7) Q: I find that my meditation is crowded with the demands of the upcoming day. Meditation becomes another demand.

   A: It would be nice to live free from demands, but still quite a bit can be experienced with the demands. Submit! Submit to the demands of the moment. Your life will be peaceful and bright if you submit to the demand first thing in the morning to pay attention to the breath and the distractions (meditation). It will be peaceful if you submit to the demand of planning your day, all thoughts on the planning. The pursuit of the demands of the day one by one without worry about the last one and the next one will produce peace. Come to think of it freedom might be defined as making a choice about to what to submit.

8) Q: (Continued) I had a period at work where the demands were so constant that for weeks I just faced one task after another without thinking about them. I was very peaceful and secure. It would be nice if that could be recreated.

A: It can be recreated. That is what we are doing in this practice. What happened to you, and has happened to me, is that the deluge of work removed time to rethink what had been done, worry about what needs to be done next, or worry about the consequences technical, political, and interpersonal of the decisions being made. Therefore, you and I lived in the moment. I received feedback from my friends, worried that I was unhappy because my affect was so low. But I was very happy. Just involved.

The trick is to create that involvement in the moment without the external assistance of great stress. Can you and I do the dishes with that concentration although we have all morning in which to get them done?

Third Interlude

Intention

I am a little shy about writing about "intention" and "will" since I have little basis for what I say but my own experience. The Buddhist masters have said nothing on the subject that has made its way through to me. At moments it seems on the matters of intention and will that they ignore the obvious. Christians have said much about will but not much that makes sense, placed in the context of meditation practice and the learning from the practice.

Nevertheless, allow me to provide a ladder, a hierarchy of the experience of intention, will, and person. I will begin with states that I consider less desirable and end with the states that I would hope for.

There is a way of being in which I am simply a response to stimuli. In that way of being, I exist without intention of my own but directed by the intentions of others. Perhaps the marketers, or the authorities, or the books, or my peers and colleagues are the closest that I can come to identifying where responsibility lies for my behavior.

In the fourth century Boethius defined a "person" as "the center of attribution of a human nature." If my actions cannot be attributed to me, I am then not a person. I might say that this appears to be the normal state for most people most of the time.

A step up the ladder is to look at all things in terms of my well being. All my intentions and all my will directs my behavior to work in my own narrow self-interest. I have not become more a person since I have simply substituted blind response to my urges for blind response to other peoples' demands. I look more a person but am not. I am only responding to the need-fulfillment side of my human nature. We refer to this as being "egotistical."

Another step up the ladder, a step to full personhood, is to distance my decision making from demands of society and urges of nature and make independent, thoughtful decisions about where and how to direct my behavior, not only for my good but for the good of the whole. At that point I am at my fullest as a person. This is the subject of C. S. Lewis's famous book *The Abolition of Man.*

This can happen at two levels. The first is to be intentional in terms of my life in general. Not accepting values willy-nilly, but intending values. Not floating in the cultural stream, but deciding my own goals. Not seduced into everyone's life style, but choosing my own.

The second level is in the minutiae of daily life. Choosing to speak or not. Choosing to have a cup of tea, or not. Choosing to stay or go. All of these little things perhaps seem to always be matters of choice, but in fact are usually matters of habit. In the process of this intentionality on the micro level, brightness infects daily tasks. Indeed, even on the general level of values, goals, and lifestyles, at a moment when an actual decision must be made, an action initiated, a direction taken that is clearly intentional, free from life pressure, at that moment brightness and clarity will emerge.

The phenomenon of brightness arises because to be intentional is to be conscious. To be habitual or unintentional is to be asleep. The inverse is also true that to be conscious is to be intentional. When we turn our life in the moment to the control of habit, we sleep. When we are intentional, we wake.

Thus we have the example of the Zen masters. First, they urge that we make life simple and be aware in the moment of what we do. This implies being intentional although they have not said that in my hearing. Second, when they report great breakthroughs of illumination, they frequently report the moment when the student stops doing what he has been told and begins doing what he wants to do.

Delightful as living this way is, more is possible. (Or to be more exact, less is possible.) In meditation practice, indeed in this book from chapter 3 on, we are urged not to identify what is happening as ours. The more one sits, the more one becomes aware that what is happening is not me. All of these thoughts and feelings have their genesis elsewhere and simply rumble through and disappear. I am a verb.

The one mention of intention I know of in Buddhist practice is the intention to be enlightened. It is "right intention" and is listed as one of the steps in the eightfold path. But how can I possess this one thing when nothing else is mine? The answer is that I do not possess "right intention" but that it too arises from the underlying unity. I do not possess right intention. It possesses me.

(It is with this intention that I look with loving awareness at all that arises, and it is because of this intention that the good tends to continue and the bad tends to fade.)

This is similar to the statement and identical to the reality that I need not desire God since God desires me. I need not struggle to posses God, because God possesses me. All I need is to become aware that the Divine possesses me. Jesus' parable of the Prodigal Son teaches that the father maintains relationship with the son no matter what the son does. All the son need do to return from loneliness and exile is to remember his relationship.

If I were to really come to this awakening, would I be more of a person, or less? I think that I will not be a person at all. Perfectly possessed by God's intentions I would no longer be the center of attribution of my nature. God would be.

Bernadette Roberts in *The Experience of No-self* says: "As I see it, a contemplative is one who is aware of this movement (God's will), striving at first to go with it, but later discovering he is being moved without effort. He abandons himself to become part of it—one with it—until finally, he realizes he has never been anything other than this movement itself."

This is the bliss of those who have "found Jesus" in some dramatic way. They are not there anymore. They are bliss and nothing else. They are not persons. The Divine has them. God is the noun. They are the verb.

For those of us in the planful religions this is frightening and indeed it has its risks. Running around with no mind could cause accidents. But even we of the major institutional religions are confronted with the question: What did Paul mean when he said that he no longer lived but Christ lived in him?

Notice that I am led to speak of "no mind," a non-state central to the Buddhist tradition. Often this is seen as quiet and empty but the emptiness is only that no ego and no person diverts the flow of the spirit of God. Intention pours forth into action. It is just not my intention, and therefore not really my action, and most certainly not I.

Is that not a courageous prayer? To lose self in the Divine? But we Christians say it half asleep every time we renew our baptismal promises. When I think this way I recognize that I have not sought this practice but it has sought me, just as I have not sought the Divine, but the Divine has sought me.

I fled him down the nights and down the days;
I fled him down the arches of the years;
I fled him, down the labyrinthian ways
Of my own mind; and in the mist of tears
I hid from him, and under running laughter.

Francis Thompson

This answers an earlier question in a different way. "Since we are not supposed to desire, how can we desire God? Or for that matter enlightenment?" No need to desire. Just stop being in the way. Desire nothing. Then you become nobody. Then God, who has always desired you, has you in her motherly embrace. Our tradition says that she says: "You are the apple of my eye. I have held you in the palm of my hand."

When the mind is in any way active, this background is "consciousness as witness," absolutely non-involved. When mental activity ceases, it is "pure objectless consciousness." This background is our true nature and can only be revealed spontaneously, i.e., in an attitude devoid of any striving, of any premeditation, any intention. This reality, being formless, escapes any qualification whatsoever. However, the traditional words "peace" and "bliss" are nearest to expressing it. This background can be perceived in each interval that occurs between two thoughts or two perceptions. In such intervals one may come upon the timeless moment, in other words, the eternal present.

Be Who You Are, Jean Klein

11

Evolution and the Reign of God

We are still looking back at the Pentecostal events in a dazed way instead of looking forward to the goal the spirit is leading us to. Therefore mankind is wholly unprepared for the things to come. Man is compelled by divine forces to go forward to increasing consciousness and cognition, developing further and further away from his religious background because he does not understand it any more. His religious leaders and teachers are still hypnotized by the beginning of a then new aeon of consciousness instead of understanding them and their implication. What was once called the 'Holy Ghost' is an impelling force creating wider consciousness and responsibility and thus enriched cognition. The real history of the world seems to be the progressive incarnation of the deity.

Carl Jung quoted in
Wounded Healer of the Soul
by Claire Dunn

Take It Seriously

Blessed be the Lord, the God of Israel,
He has come to his people and set them free.
He has raised up for us a mighty savior,
Born of the house of his servant David. . . .
In the tender compassion of our God,
The dawn from on high shall break upon us,
To shine on those who dwell in darkness and the shadow of
    death,
And to guide our feet into the way of peace."

Explanation

Jesus never thought of himself in the context of the eons of human evolution. The scholars are certain that he saw himself as a man addressing those right in front of him on issues that they faced right then. He did not look back to see himself as the culmination of Jewish history. (Early Christians did that for him and then put the words on his lips.) He did not look ahead ten years to prophesy, much less two centuries or two millennia. The reason his words have meaning to us is not that they were addressed to us but that in meeting immediate needs he spoke so profoundly that the words had meaning for the centuries.

Despite the fact that past and future were not his perspective, we who have scientific verification that the world has evolved and is continuing to evolve, can and should study our traditions to see if they make more or less sense in the light of the hypothesis of evolution.

Certainly, when evolution first ran up against religious tradition, we were terrified and saw this thinking as challenge only. We thought it something to be faced down. We attacked and defended. But by the mid-fifties the writings of the French Jesuit paleontologist, Teilhard de Chardin began to integrate religious tradition and evolution in a manner that diminished neither and enhanced both. What follows in this chapter although not directly quoted from him is reliant on his research and reasoning.

The Hebrew shepherds that founded Jesus' nation told a story of the beginning of the world, later recorded in the first book of the canonical Bible, the book of Genesis. The written story is nearly three thousand years old, and the spoken story came much earlier than that. The story is:

> God created the world and breathed his own life into two of the creatures of this world. These people, the parents of the rest of humanity, were given dominion over all that was and were destined to live a life of total happiness, even meeting with God in the garden in the evening to chat about the affairs

of the day. However, when offered the one thing God forbade, the fruit of the tree of the knowledge of good and evil, they fell to temptation. Because of that fall these two humans were exiled from the garden, had to work for a living, and fell prey to illness and death.

The story, of course is fiction, not history; poetry, not science. What the many authors were trying to convey is that the existential situation in which they found themselves was not God's fault. The good came from God. What blame there was should fall on us. Their intent was not to say *when* it happened but in allegorical fashion to explain what was true at the time they lived. At the same time they compared what was true then to what God was really trying to create.

What if the state that the authors speak of as the original state, is not the beginning, but a preconscious intuition of the future? What if the paradise they were describing was the reign of God that Jesus experienced, and what if that reign of God over eons could be extended to all creatures? What happens when we pull out the threads of this story and reweave it as a portrait of what is to come? What if instead of visualizing God as an old man with a beard we visualized God as the underlying power of all that seems to be happening, a power that appears to be striving in a direction.

The secular word for God's presence and God's life is "consciousness." I hesitate to use the word because while it makes some things clear, it is too mild a word for the force, power, person, that I and my companions and my forbears in all the religious traditions of this earth have sensed and in some cases met.

If I were to ask my friend whose chest split open if what he had experienced was consciousness, I think he would find the word inadequate. Martin Luther did not think to use it, nor did Paul the apostle, nor did Jesus of Nazareth. The force they experienced acted with a sense of direction.

What must be added to the secular picture to bring it in line with the sacred reality is the presence in that consciousness of an immense reservoir of love. Define "love" for this moment as "intention for the good." That word added and the Hebrew God emerges, the Father of Jesus' understanding, a divine stream of loving consciousness, loving awareness, loving attention that not only creates the world but seeks to explode into the world through those of us willing to empty ourselves.

So, for our understanding, much as the patriarch could not look at the face of God so God only showed him his back, let us use "loving consciousness" as the back of the Divine Presence.

Then I can say that not only is loving consciousness the cause, but it was loving consciousness that our early parents received, loving consciousness that was nurtured, loving consciousness that has been evolving, and loving consciousness that is preparing to take over the earth. As Jung says in the passage quoted above: "The real history of the world seems to be the progressive incarnation of the deity."

The scientific perspective is developed in *The Phenomena of Man* by de Chardin. To speak simply of his theory, for my own scientific background is weak, he says that when he studies the flow of evolution starting from prehistoric times he sees two phenomena.

First, things move from simple to complex. They remain simple organisms until they reach the limits of whatever container they are in, from a drop of water, to a puddle, to a land mass. Then they turn back towards one another, join together, and become a more complex organism. This pattern endures from the tiniest microscopic being, through to mammals.

Second, what distinguishes one degree of complexity from its predecessor, other than complexity itself, is consciousness. Each succeeding step produces more self-direction and more self-awareness. It appears as if underlying the process is a greater force moving toward the end state of more consciousness. So much so that while this force appears to experiment with various forms at each level, once greater consciousness has been achieved the experiment at that level ends and begins at the next level of potential sophistication.

Chardin sees humanity as the present end state of the process, and he sees in the fact that we have reached the limits of our container, the earth, and are being forced inward towards one another as the next step in evolution. He expects that in our enforced unity we will move closer to the end point to which this greater force is pressing and guiding us. Conflict and war are but byproducts of God's primordial push toward greater consciousness, or as Jung put it, toward the incarnation of the Divine.

Our Hebrew forebears, eons ago, woke to the realization that something different than simple animal response could direct their lives. Speaking still of the back of the Divine Presence, I shall say that they woke to loving consciousness. But not as simply the fact that they were conscious, but beyond that, they attributed their own consciousness to consciousness itself that extends beyond them.

Unlike every other tribe of their time, and every other people for millennia, they rejected the theory that this loving consciousness was scattered phenomena at war even with itself lying behind the existence of many animals and things, a multiplicity of gods. They said that this phenomena is one God, one loving consciousness, that has created all, but flows into the earth now primarily through human beings, those made in his image and likeness.

This Hebrew tribe knows something that the rest of the world does not:

> He makes his word known to Jacob,
> To Israel his laws and decrees—
> He has not dealt thus with other nations,
> He has not taught them his commands. (Ps 147)

That knowledge shall be spread to all the earth through the instrumentality of Jesus and his company. As the prophet, priest, and father Zechariah sings at the birth of his son, John the Baptist:

> Blessed be the Lord, the God of Israel,
> He has come to his people and set them free.

He has raised up for us a mighty savior,
Born of the house of his servant David. . . .
In the tender compassion of our God,
The dawn from on high shall break upon us,
To shine on those who dwell in darkness and the shadow of
    death,
And to guide our feet into the way of peace."

The simple path to a present salvation given in our religious literature, the Bible, is to abandon ourselves to the will of the Father. The book of Genesis traces our fall to eating of the tree of the Knowledge of Good and Evil. This is to take on ourselves the judgment as to what is good and evil. The path of abandonment to God's will is to reverse the failure at the foot of the tree: leave to God to decide what is good and evil, and submit. For those of us who follow Jesus of Nazareth the symbol of this submission is the tree of the cross.

". . . He humbled himself, and became obedient to the point of death—even the death on a cross. Therefore God also highly exalted him and gave him the name that is above very name . . ." Philippians

You and I can join this great flow of life sitting quietly in our chairs, conscious of our breath, conscious of our body, conscious of the reality around us, conscious of our own loving consciousness, perhaps even aware of the great presence of loving consciousness itself lurking beyond the narrow door, making no judgment. Simply sitting. Sitting simply. Not for us to decide what is good and what is evil. Simply to live with what God has given us. And that is glory.

This practice begins before us and goes beyond us. Those willing to do this, in quiet triumph, lead the course of evolution, prepare the way for a new generation, and open the door to a greater reality. This practice is created by a force greater than us and creates a being greater than any one of us.

When the door opens for humanity, the world, the universe, I doubt that we will call it consciousness, or even loving consciousness. The word is too small. Perhaps we will call it "Wonderful," or "The Prince of Peace," or even "Mighty God."

When that door opens, I suspect we shall think we have walked into the kingdom of God. We shall experience the fact that Meister Eckhart's Son of God dwells in us. We shall bow to one another saying: *Namaste.* We shall address the heavens with: *Alleluia.* But let us wait for that time and see.

In an opening chapter I talked about the need to pray always and have mentioned it little since. I have not emphasized constant prayer partly because I am learning/teaching from the Buddha, and the Buddhist do not think of God as a separate being, and therefore there is not difference between awareness of self and awareness of God. So I have emphasized awareness generally and not awareness of God.

A second reason for this de-emphasis is that I fear that we Christians too quickly leap to concepts, and if I speak about prayer to God too soon or too often the average Christian will begin addressing words (concepts) to some dim idea (concept) of God. Any idea of God is a delusion. We cannot know God. The ancient Israelite would not speak God's name that he not be confused into thinking he knew God. It is "idolatry" to conceptualize God for then we adore a concept and not God. There is no adequate concept for God.

Once we have learned to be aware of whatever is there to be aware of, and aware of ourselves as aware and conscious beings, we can quietly direct our attention to that deep and imponderable Ground of Being that we rest in, the Divine Presence. Thomas Kelly, a Quaker, refers to it as living in the light *(A Testament of Devotion).* See if it too comes to our awareness, and if not, let it rest for another day. In time it will.

Pray always. It appears to be the final step or at least the next step in the evolutionary path planted in our genes, and the genetic code of creation. We are to chat with God in the garden in the evening. We are to bear his being in our bones. We are the conscious voice of the Divine Presence in the universe. Our prayer is

God's prayer. When we humans were primitive, before we became sophisticated, we knew how to do this. Once again, salvation is a return to the perspective of childhood with adult eyes.

Brother Lawrence in the *Practice of the Presence of God* says that "I make it my business only to persevere in his holy presence, wherein I keep myself by a simple attention, and a general fond regard of God, which I may call an actual presence of God. . . ."

A simple man gives us a simple task. He lived in a monastery filled with philosophers, theologians, and other scholars and has outlasted all his degreed brothers in Christ as a teacher to the ages. He was the cook.

I think the Buddha would understand that the monastery should listen to the cook. I know Jesus had a profound regard for cooks and other lowly people. So I end here.

UU (THE BOTTOM LINE)

By sitting with loving attention we join the flow of God's evolutionary power.

It is not that we know for sure. History is still unfolding. What this all means will not become clear until the last line is written. We see now as through a glass, darkly. "The dawn from on high shall break upon us." For now we work with hypotheses in an attempt to understand. As A. N. Whitehead said about his own work, "It's a likely story." What more can we ask?

Practical Matters

A last look at that thing we call "loving attention" before ending. It is not the same as the normal attention we give to things, or even thoughts and feelings. "Loving attention" is aware of the attending self at the same time as it is aware of whatever it is looking at.

That attending self is the quiet place that lives only in the now and desires nothing that is not now present. It is Klein's background that observes objects without moving, and becomes in the absence of the object pure objectless consciousness itself. Meister Eckhart refers to it as an immutable place. It is the place in me that is not moved, desires not motion, desires only what is given. Meister Eckhart says that when we live from that place, we are like God in that we see all things changing and are not changed ourselves.

Eckhart was not a tower mystic. He was an administrator in the Dominican order with responsibilities for places and people. He was not too busy for this practice.

This immutable place is then a place that can be carried anywhere. Meister Eckhart says so. He did it. While his body rushed from location to location his heart was still. He lived in the Divine Presence. I pray the same for you, and I ask the same for me.

Questions and Answers:

1) **Q:** I have found that this practice helps me with life in that I am more detached from outcomes, much calmer about decisions, and much better at making them. I thought the point was to live in the kingdom of God, not be a business success.

   A: Lots of points to anything. Being a business success is not what we are about, but now that I know I have helped you do that, remind me to charge extra. Many of the masters focus much more on this practice as an aid to "skillful living" than I have. There are simple answers easily noticed by one on this path that people living more frantically just don't see.

2) **Q:** I find myself smiling during meditation with a sense of contentment about where and who I am. Is that normal? All right to do?

   A: Some teachers recommend smiling while sitting, plastering the smile on the face even when not feeling it, to induce the proper feeling of meditation, something like what you feel. The smile indicates the loving awareness, the loving acceptance, loving consciousness of what is flowing through.

3) Q: I find the sitting practice very helpful. I find the essays interesting but not all that central to what I am doing. Often I find the questions and answers much too philosophical. Is this a problem?

A: See next answer.

4) Q: Being "in Christ" is different than experiencing the Divine Presence is it not?

A: The answer to both of these questions hinges on the difference between dualism and non-dualism.

Answering question three, if we are a seamless universe (non-dualism), then whatever avenue we take to becoming aware will bring us to the Divine Presence. Some of us just sit and see what comes up. Some of us as well as sitting puzzle about the nature of what is happening. In case you have not noticed, I am one of the latter. But if you just sit you will experience what is there and if I sit and puzzle, I will experience what is there. The biggest mistake is to let the puzzling get in the way of the sitting because it is in the sitting that the experience arises, not in the puzzling.

However as a puzzler, I deeply appreciate your questions. You have helped me immensely. I am envious of those who feel no need to puzzle. I cannot tell you how many times I suspect that the vision of God faded because having it created an extremely bright idea in my mind, which quickly stepped between the vision and me.

Answering question 4, if we are a seamless universe, (non-dualism) then we really can't be anything without being everything. So if we are in Christ, we are in the Divine Presence, or if we are really aware of ourselves, we are aware of being in Christ and in the Divine Presence.

Part of the difficulty of understanding is that we Christians put specifically Christian labels on experiences. I think we can excuse our Jewish-Christian forebears. When they announced the primacy of Jesus, they were not comparing themselves to the Buddha but to the Roman Emperor. Without the Internet they were necessarily chauvinist in their religious perspective. We do not have this excuse.

The experience of being in Christ is the experience of being one with all other Christians, including Jesus of Nazareth. But all that really is, is the experience of being one with the universe, which we have limited to the experience of being a Christian.

Thomas Merton, the famous Trappist monk, author, and mystic, experienced his great epiphany, not in the abbey church, not in his hermitage, but while waiting on a street corner in the local town for a doctor's appointment. He experienced the Divine in seeing people, shopping, hustling, selling, and driving. Now, all of that did not happen irrespective of the fact that he had done one heck of a lot of meditating, praying, singing, reading, writing, and puzzling. That helped him greatly.

When he experienced this unity with all as Divine he did not do a survey to isolate the Christians from anyone else who happen to be in the vicinity. He felt his unity with all. What made it Christian was that he was a Christian.

That is not to say that around the corner there may not have been a twenty-four-year-old atheistic hooker without a high school diploma having the same experience as she poured the last bottle of scotch she ever planned to drink into the gutter.

5) Q: What connection do you see between meditation and spiritual direction? A number of people I have met who have a meditation practice seem to have a mentor or a spiritual director. What is the connection? Is it necessary?

A: Most of the Buddhist teachers, with a couple of exceptions, are insistent on the need for a teacher and by that they do not mean someone functioning as loosely as I function, but somebody right on top of you and your practice. That is because delusion is a tricky adversary. You can be fooled easily.

However, the state of spiritual direction in our church is questionable. My experience is that those claiming to do it do not know what they are doing. Everybody is fumbling. So what is the gain of having someone like that chatting with you? It is not the same as having a Buddhist master who has ground this into his or her bones. What follows may be a testimonial to my limited experience. But I have read a couple of books and had three directors and have no idea what they are about. So I'd say it's a great idea if you can find somebody who knows what they are doing.

In the meantime chatting about it with a friend might be helpful. This is not simply a semantic distinction. A friend is a fellow fumbler. A spiritual director should have the bone-deep knowledge you need. Some in this business are recognizing this distinction and referring to themselves as spiritual "friends" instead of spiritual "directors." I would prefer that instead of downgrading the title they upgrade the service.

If I was called to submit a summary judgment, I would say that most of them accept delusion as if it were reality. They then help a person live with delusion. Not the point, it seems to me.

Postlude on the Christian Life

The superconsciousness which is possessed by man as long as he is created in God's image cannot be separable from the relative sensuous consciousness which performs most useful functions in this world of particulars. The superconsciousness must be thoroughly and in the most perfect manner interfused with the one in daily use; otherwise, the superconsciousness cannot be of any significance to us. It is indeed so interfused with our psychological consciousness that we are utterly unconscious of its presence. It requires certain spiritual training to be awakened to it, and it is Zen that has for the first time in the world history of mental evolution pointed out this fact. In a word, it is Zen that has become aware of the truth of superconsciousness in connection with the most commonplace doings in our daily life.

The Threefold Question in Zen, D. T. Suzuki

Jesus gave us himself as an example of constant prayer. But most of his stories are about how to live the life of the kingdom, assuming that if we but live that life, we will come to see the reign of God unfolding in front of us.

Meister Eckhart distinguishes three steps on the path to full union with God. The first is the *rapturous* experience of understanding that the Divine Presence lives in me. A moment of loving attention, one might say. The second is the *ongoing* experience that the Divine Presence lives in me. Learning to pray always throughout the interactions of daily life. This is "mindful living" in the terms of *vipassana* meditation. The third is the realization that *everything* is the Divine Presence. We live within the Divine Presence, so to speak.

A student of mine passed on a story told by a teacher who used gongs to stimulate meditation. He enjoyed doing this with smaller children, five-year-olds or so. He would encourage them to follow the ringing of the gong deep into themselves as far as it would go. What fun to hear their answers to the question of what had happened to them while chasing the sound.

He reports one little girl who seemed quite taken with the experiment but was having difficulty answering adult questions about what had happened during the few minutes of childish meditation. Finally an adult asked, "Did you see God?"

"No," she laughed with evident joy that the words had finally come to her and she could now be a good child and give an answer to attentive adults, "No, I didn't *see* God," she said, "I *was* God."

Jesus said that it is to those who think like these children that the reign of God will be evident. The Divine Presence in me meets the Divine Presence in you. Loving consciousness meeting loving consciousness. When you see Hindus folding their hands and giving those dinky little bows to one another, the word they utter under their breath is *namaste* or "I salute the Divine Presence in you."

When I was a young man, on a dreary evening in March, I went for a five-mile run. On the way out, in my sadness, I found my lips moving to the rhythm of my feet with the words "A distant God and a lonely man." On the return, I noticed that without my noticing the words had changed to "A lonely God and a distant man."

UU (THE BOTTOM LINE)

"The Father's imperial rule is like a merchant who had a supply of merchandise and then found a pearl. That merchant was prudent and he sold the merchandise and bought the single pearl for himself" (9) This book exists to introduce you to the kingdom of God. All else is meaningless in comparison.

Practical Matters

The point of the practice has been, of course, to practice for ordinary life. By now it would not be uncommon for you to have moments of deep awareness of the Divine Presence in daily life. Some places and times are more conducive than others are. A place I find conducive to awareness is in the store shopping for groceries with the deluxe smells and sights of the store and people focused on their own tasks, requiring nothing of me, allowing me to see them in their glory. The trick is to refuse to look at the world with the world's mindset, but to look at the world with understanding that it is the reign of God in disguise. Loving attention blows the dust of delusion from the glory of reality.

Yesterday I sat in the lunch area at Target, eating a personal pizza, savoring the beauty of my inner city neighborhood in all its colors and shapes shopping. I was deeply aware of humanity as odd vessels carrying God.

Pin to the frame of your outer door, Brother Lawrence's prayer:

O my God, since Thou art with me, and I must now, in obedience to Thy commands, apply my mind to those outward things, I beseech Thee to grant me the grace to continue in Thy presence, and to this end do Thou prosper me with Thy assistance, receive all my works, and possess all my affections.

Questions and Answers

1) Q: Didn't you find being a rector in a parish difficult granted the various stages of spiritual development in people?

A: The Buddha was quite clear on the role of good behavior in the development of the spiritual life. Do good stuff. You become better. Don't do good stuff, and you may meditate until hell freezes over without improving. Most parishes focus on the level of good behavior almost exclusively, and that was an annoyance for me as rector. I would have liked more people to surge to my meditation classes, my reflective writing class, my Bible study. But some did. Enough came that I was pleased and happy.

People loved each other, for the most part. Not much gossiping. Not any more than I was perfectly comfortable partaking in from time to time. Much hugging. Much delight in one another's presence. Pleasant potluck dinners. Warm and friendly liturgies. When one old lady broke her leg six hundred miles from home and could not get onto an airplane, three men from the parish rented a van and drove to retrieve her.

I would have liked more focus on the inner life from my parish and tried to bring it. But I was not ready to drive 1,200 miles in service of my neighbor. So I do not plan to criticize them greatly. As I said earlier: "The practice of giving readily provides a sacramental (something that causes what it signifies) tool for releasing my grasp on my sense of person and allowing the Spirit of the Father to take over my being." Meditation is not the only formative tool available to a Christian. Giving by cooking for the youth breakfast or organizing the rummage sale or working for Habitat for Humanity have their role and for some personality types they are more readily helpful than sitting.

2) Q: What would you recommend a parish do to come more in line with this kind of thinking?

A: Put a daily hour of prayer and meditation in the pastor's job description. Hold her or him to the task of becoming a spiritual giant. Do whatever it takes to make it easier for the pastor to do this. I ran a small parish and, as you might suspect, I had a huge commitment to this practice. Even so, heading to the sanctuary with the snow not shoveled, or the youth room filthy, or the bulletin not folded was difficult. Get the pastor competent support so his or her focus can be on the spirit.

Hire a youth minister or get a volunteer to cover that function. A good youth minister really enjoys hayrides, bowling leagues, water pistols, and emotional breakdowns around campfires. The odds that the same person will make a pastor for adults are zero to less. Sure the pastor should get along famously with the kids. I got along famously with the kids but that was because they appreciated the fact that the person their parents reverenced took each and every one of them seriously by name. They also knew who they wanted to go skiing with and confide their troubles to, and that was the youth minister, not me.

Take a look at the role of a Hasidic rabbi. There is the kind of expectation that demands greatness. The Hasidic congregation treats its rabbi with enormous respect. The pope has more devotees surrounding him but not more intense devotion. The catch is, that the rabbi better well live up to what they are respecting him for. He is on the hook. The path of early (Theravadan) Buddhism was that the spiritual leader was to seek personal holiness and the rest of the people would follow.

Start a meditation class, a Bible study, or some such, and keep it running and obvious despite the fact not many come. In time it will grow if it deserves to.

Find something in between this rather rigorous practice and potluck dinners to fit the needs of people who are not like you and I, desperate for the truth, but would still like to go deeper.

One pastor I know offers people the opportunity to take vows in three areas: Prayer, study, and compassion. People take one vow in each area. People can get help from him or in a group for formulating the promise. Then they write it down and mail it to him to file. If they want, he will read their vow. If they want, he will review their progress on their vow. Some just make their vows and don't even mail them in. The vow lasts a year, and then if the person wishes a new set can be made. This priest thinks that this program or non-program is working to make his parish vital and growing. Seems likely. His parish is vital and growing, and he is not a dramatic charismatic figure.

Don't start feeling elitist about meditation practice. I am pleased that you have entered it. I think everyone should. But I also think everyone should be willing to drive 1,200 miles to pick up nice old ladies with broken legs, and I have not yet entered that practice. And I think everyone should.

3) Q: I have recently decided that church is not all that important, and with that I suddenly found that I found it quite helpful. Make sense?

A: Certainly. Instead of measuring the Church against a high standard, you can now take what it actually has to offer. Read about the first disciples and see if we have gotten any worse than they were. What a bunch! The old rector at a parish I attended used to say: "If you think me a hypocrite for claiming Christian ideals and still being a poor human being, just think how rotten I would be if I did not claim the ideals." The Church can be a vehicle for moving toward the kingdom. Getting on the train does not mean you have arrived, nor does it mean the train has arrived. You are still in process as it is in process.

4) Q: I believe I have had moments when I was really awake and free of delusion. One sign is that I have a moment of panic when it happens, then everything turns bright with rich colors. But this lasts only a few seconds and then does not return for months. Can I cause this to happen more often?

A: You really do not cause anything and trying will screw your head up. However, having been awake you now know when you are asleep. Simply become aware with loving attention that you are asleep. Frequently the fact that you are aware wakes you up.

5) Q: I find that the world is always trying to reinforce my sense of person, what you called my "social self." I feel like I am losing the battle. The other day I had to tell my husband to stop trying to define me. Five minutes from now I may want to be somebody else. Any advice?

A: First, I think you are winning the battle. If you notice that you are being defined, that is a remarkable step. And then to tell your husband is impressive. And then the fact that he did not run screaming from the house is an added plus saying quite a bit about him, and your relationship.

The problem is that the closest we can come to not being a person is in complete isolation, silence, and inactivity, which of course, is impossible. There is always something going on. When I try to do something, I must become a person to do it. Indeed, if we hope to have impact, we need to seek training, practice, support systems, and roles, and with that come most of the trappings of personhood. The Scripture scholars say that it was when the message of the free spirit, Jesus, hit the reality of householders wanting to take it in, at that point it was radically adapted, changed beyond recognition. People who were trying to live a "normal" life could not lose their sense of person.

Only a few of us have the privilege of the solitary life free from the constraints of personhood. These people are called "monks" from the Greek *monos* meaning someone alone and isolated.

However, be aware that the social self rises in response to a sense of connection to other people. For this reason, Jesus tells us to hate our relatives. Observe your feelings of connection. You are not connected, so if you observe you will notice that connection is a delusion. If you do not feel connected your husband's words will not affect you. You do not need to fix him if you will fix yourself.

6)   Q: Is this not Quietism? Are we not seeking the annihilation of the will? Simply sitting and watching delusion pass by.

A: No, I scream, no, no, no.

The question makes me want to burn my own book. I am horrified to have misled you so badly and grateful that you asked. And hope that anyone so misled reads this very last question and answer.

I am a Christian, and even worse, an Anglican. Anglican theology is for the best part poetry about ordinary life. We see the Divine in the ordinary. (If in no other place, you experienced Anglican theology when you took English literature in high school.) Our problem has been a refusal to look for the Divine in spiritual practice. We have not looked for the quiet place and have been captivated by the hectic. What I do here is redress the balance. These pages try to separate the divine Presence as an experience in my soul from feelings, thoughts, culture, fear, pain, and even my sense of being a person, so that I come aware of the Divine peace and light within me. But I do not want to simply sit with this awareness. I want the Divine to suffuse my feelings, thoughts, desires, and even that person that I create as I move into action. I want to become more vigorous, not less, with a divine vigor. More aware of life passing, not less, with a divine awareness. More willful, not less, with not my will, but that of the Father who sent me.

I suppose I have failed in these pages to communicate this clearly. In the excitement of the retreat into the depths of being, I suspect I denigrate the outward flow into action. My apologies.

My Bookshelf

The book you have read is the work of a parish priest functioning as a parish priest does. I have been slow to cite specific authors as sources for specific statements because a parish priest's task is to seek knowledge from authorities, bring it into his or her own heart, and then replay it as his or her own knowledge. For if it has been truly brought to heart, it is truly my knowledge, and I no longer can safely attribute it to another. Indeed, those others might find it irritating to see their doctrines mixed with other peoples' ideas, shaken in my heart and then spilled forth as theirs.

So what I can do for you is give you the books sitting on the top row of my bookshelf, those most relevant to this work. You may well want to read them and allow them into your heart, that you might shake them up and pour them out as your knowledge.

"**" Indicates a book at the heart of this discussion.

"*" Indicates a book directly relevant to this discussion.

" " Indicates a book impinging on but not central to this discussion.

**Almaas, A. H. *The Point of Existence.* Berkely: Diamond Books, 1995.

Arasteh, A. Reza. *Final Integration in the Adult Personality.* Leiden: E. J. Brill, 1965.

Barfield, Owen. *Saving the Appearances.* Hanover: Wesleyan University Press. 1988.

*Becker, Ernest. *The Denial of Death.* New York: Free Press, 1973.

*Borg, Marcus J. *Jesus a New Vision*. San Francisco: Harper SanFrancisco, 1987.

**Borg, Marcus J. *Meeting Jesus Again for the First Time*. San Francisco: HarperSanFrancisco, 1994.

Buber, Martin. *I and Thou*. New York: Simon and Schuster, 1996.

**Burtt, E. A., (ed.) *The Teachings of the Compassionate Buddha*. New York: Mentor Books, 1982.

*Chardin, Teilhard de. *The Future of Man*. New York: Harper and Row, 1964.

**Chardin, Teilhard de. *The Phenomenon of Man*. New York: Harper Torchbooks, 1965.

Chetwynd, Tom. *Zen and the Kingdom of Heaven*. Boston: Wisdom Publications, 2001.

*Crossan, John Dominic. *The Historical Jesus*. San Francisco: HarperSanFrancisco, 1991.

Culligan, Kevin, et al. *Purifying the Heart*. New York: Crossroad, 1994.

Dalai Lama. *How to Practice*. New York: Pocket Books, 2002.

*Fleischman, Paul. *Karma and Chaos*. Seattle: Vipassana Research Publication, 1999.

**Forman, Robert K. C. *Meister Eckhart, Mystic as Theologian*. Rockport: Element, 1991.

Freke, Thomas, and Peter Gandy. *The Jesus Mysteries*. New York: Three Rivers Press, 1999.

Funk, Robert W., et al. *The Acts of Jesus*. San Francisco: HarperSanFrancisco, 1998.

**Funk, Robert W., et al. *The Five Gospels*. New York: Scribner, 1996.

**Funk, Robert W., et al. *The Gospel of Jesus*. Santa Rosa: Polebridge, 1999.

**Gunaratana, Henepola. *Mindfulness in Plain English*. Boston: Wisdom, 1991.

**Hart, William. *Vipassana Meditation as Taught by S. N. Goenka*. New York: Harper and Row, 1991.

Keating, Thomas. *The Kingdom of God is Like . . . .* New York: Cross Road, 1997.

**Kelly, Thomas R. *A Testament of Devotion.* San Francisco: Harper, 1992.

**Klein, Jean. *Who am I ?.* Rockport: Element, 1988.

**Klein, Jean. *Be Who You Are.* London: Watkins, 1973.

**Brother Lawrence. *The Practice of the Presence of God.* White Plains: Peter Pauper, 1963.

Morinaga, Soko. *Novice to Master.* Boston: Wisdom Publications, 2002.

Meyer, Marvin trans. *The Gospel of Thomas.* San Francisco: HarperSanFrancisco, 1992.

*Meister Eckhart, *Essential Sermons.* New York: Paulist Press, 1981.

*Merton, Thomas. *Zen and the Birds of Appetite.* New York: New Directions, 1968.

Merton, Thomas. *The Way of Chuang Tzu.* New York: New Directions, 1965.

Newberg, Andrew, et al. *Why God Won't Go Away.* New York: Ballantine Books, 2001.

*O'Neal, David, ed. *Meister Eckhart from Whom God Hid Nothing.* Boston: Shambahla, 1996.

Pennington, Basil, *Centering Prayer,* Image Book.

Rinpoche, Thrangu. *Everyday Consciousness and Buddha Awakening.* New York: Snow Lion Publications, 2002.

**Roberts, Bernadette. *The Experience of No-self.* Boulder and London: Shambhala, 1984.

*Sinetar, Marsha. *Ordinary People as Monks and Mystics.* New York: Paulist Press, 1986.

Suzuki, D. T., et al. *Zen Buddhism and Psychoanalysis.* New York: Grove, 1963.

*Suzuki, D. T. *Introduction to Zen Buddhism.* New York: Grove, 1964.

*Suzuki, D. T. *The Awakening of Zen.* Boston and London: Shambhala, 2000.

*Suzuki, Shunryu. *Zen Mind, Beginners Mind.* New York: Weatherhill, 2000.

**Thera, Nyanaponika. *The Heart of Buddhist Meditation.* York Beach: Samuel Weiser, 1965.

**Tolle, Eckhart. *The Power of Now.* Novato: New World Library, 1999.

*Watts, Alan. *The Art of Contemplation.* New York: Pantheon, 1972.

Watts, Alan. *Tao: The Watercourse Way.* New York: Pantheon, 1975.

*Wegner, Michael. Ed. *Wind Bell.* Berkely: North Atlantic Books, 2002.

*Whitehead, Alfred. *Process and Reality.* New York: The Free Press, 1978.

Wilbur, Ken. *The Marriage of Sense and Soul.* New York Broadway Books, 1999.

*Wilbur, Ken. *No Boundary.* Boston and London: Shambhala, 1985.

Index